THOUGHTS OF A FRIED CHICKEN WATERMELON WOMAN

Karen Ford

TotalRecall Publications, Inc.
1103 Middlecreek
Friendswood, Texas 77546
281-992-3131 281-482-5390 Fax
www.totalrecallpress.com

All rights reserved. Except as permitted under the United States Copyright Act of 1976, No part of this publication may be reproduced, stored in a retrieval system, or transmitted in any form or by any means electronic or mechanical or by photocopying, recording, or otherwise without prior permission of the publisher. Exclusive worldwide content publication / distribution by TotalRecall Publications, Inc.

Copyright © 2014 by: Karen Ford
All rights reserved

ISBN: 978-1-59095-574-1
UPC: 6-43977-45749-3

Printed in the United States of America with simultaneous printing in Australia, Canada, and United Kingdom.

FIRST EDITION
1 2 3 4 5 6 7 8 9 10

The scanning, uploading and distribution of this book via the Internet or via any other means without the permission of the publisher is illegal and punishable by law. Please purchase only authorized electronic editions, and do not participate in or encourage electronic piracy of copyrighted materials. Your support of the author's rights is appreciated.

**To the fried chicken
watermelon women everywhere**

Author Bio

World-Renowned Author Karen Ford has been a freelance journalist over 20 years and written for a number of local, national and international publications including the Chicago Tribune, Chicago Parent magazine, the Citizen Newspapers, Screen Magazine and Lutheran Woman Today. Her corporate clients have included the University of Illinois, the Chicago Labor Education Project, the Illinois Business Development Authority and the Women in Business Yellow Pages. She has written political ad copy for several local and county candidates and co-authored the book "Get That Cutie in Commercials."

She lives in Chicago with her family.

About The Book

This book is one Black woman's thoughts on issues of the day. Black men in academia like Dr. Cornel West or activists like Rev. Al Sharpton and Rev. Jesse Jackson, Jr. are often asked about the Black community and how the Black community views issues like the Stand Your Ground laws. None of those gentlemen speaks for me or others I know in my community. So I wrote this book to offer a more realistic view on issues like Stand Your Ground laws, the prison industrial complex and others.

Some of these are controversial. Some are reflective and still others are personal. They are written to spur conversation, inspire thought and hopefully lead to action.

Table of Contents

Author Bio IV
About The Book V
Preface VIII
Introduction XI

Part 1 LIVING COLORED IN A PASTEL WORLD   1
   White Privilege 2
   Immigrant Nation 5
   The Eye of the Beholder 9
   Intentional Inequity 14
   Lessons of the Housewives 18
   I Love Me Some Black Men 22
   Worthless 26
   House Negroes vs. Field Negroes 28
   Black Enough 31
   The All-American Kid Next Door 33
   The Great White Hope…Revisited 35
   Say It Loud! I'm Black and I'm Proud 37

Part 2 IN CONTROL & OUT OF BOUNDS   41
   Be Afraid. Be Very Afraid. 42
   It's All about Control 46
   The Terminator and the World to Come 51
   Let's Chat about Church 53
   Happy Devil's Day! 56
   Paying the Cost to be the Boss 60
   Adding Insult to Injury 63
   Sex vs. Violence 66

Part 3 NO ONE GETS OUT ALIVE   71
   Our Children, Our Loss 72
   Step Away from the Self-Help Aisle and Help Yourself.......76
   Let's Talk…To Each Other...79
   50 Shades of Crap..82
   Public Transportation..85
   Marriage Ain't for the Faint of Heart...88
   Sports Widow 92
   My Dilemma 95
   The Question is Not What Would Jesus Do? 97
   Grandma..99
   My Friend, Death 102

Acknowledgment   107

Preface

Be who you are and say what you feel because those who mind don't matter and those who matter don't mind."
--Dr. Seuss

"In order for you to insult me I would first have to value your opinion."
--Anonymous

There is wit and wisdom in both these quotes. They are two of my favorites that I use often.

In this world of social media, everyone feels the need to make their every movement known. At any given time, you can read about someone walking a dog and hearing about the dog barking at the squirrels in the park or the pretty flowers in the garden. This is not my idea of something worth sharing yet many spend an inordinate amount of time reading and writing about such things. Not me. Life is too short and there is too much to do. Why would I willingly spend time engaging about things I could care less? I don't get it and that's why I love the quote about mind over matter.

What matters to me is whether or not my voice is being heard. What matters is whether or not I can affect change in my world in my lifetime. What matters is if I can get you to think and feel and speak and do something.

Opinions don't faze me in the least. If they did, I would write a journal instead of a book. What matters is your opinion of yourself and whether that opinion will spur you to say something, change something, do something.

This book began as a way to shut my husband up.

Every time we saw something controversial on the news, we'd have a no-holds barred conversation about the topic. Then he'd tell me to put it on the internet. "Say something about this!" he'd yell and I would say okay, I'll do it. The next day or the next week, something else would come up and we'd repeat our discussion. After more than a couple of years of these conversations I decided I would finally do as he asked and post our thoughts on the internet. Suddenly I had a blog.

Blogging gave me the opportunity of not only offering my thoughts on controversial issues but to also give a voice to the folks who we almost never hear from – seasoned (read middle aged) Black women.

Women of an indiscriminate age are seen as faceless, sexless shapes with almost no value save being wives, mothers, caregivers or comic punch lines. But it's even worse for Black women. There is no place for us in film or television. (It's ironic that the only middle aged Black woman prevalent in film today is actually portrayed by a man.) With the exception of traditional gospel music, we're not part of the music industry. We're not broadcast or print reporters or columnists. Other than Maya Angelou, Terri MacMillan and Toni Morrison, we're not widely read. So we remain voiceless.

The other side is that the average Black person in

America is voiceless as well. When a subject pertaining to Black people comes up, media people reach out to Dr. Cornel West or Rev. Jesse Jackson or Rev. Al Sharpton. Not to denigrate these gentlemen but they do not speak for me or the millions of Americans like me. We are not a monolithic people and I, for one, take great offense at being treated as such.

When a tornado strikes a small town or when someone shoots up a school, reporters talk to the victims. They speak with the people involved. They don't call their stock individuals who speak for the White folks involved. Why should it be any different for Black people?

In the next pages you'll find my thoughts about subjects as mundane as motherhood and as charged as race. My thoughts range from the silly to the serious to the sublime. Some of it will be pretty and some of it will not. Some of it may be seen as sacrilegious and some of it will appear as pious. However they may seem the thoughts spoken are my own as honest and clear as possible.

Laugh cry, scream, curse but whatever you think, think and then do something. I ask no less of me and no more of you.

Introduction

My dear departed friend, Eyvonne, used to tell the story of being in the grocery store one morning when a man walked up to her and said "Girl, you remind me of fried chicken and watermelon." Being the diplomatic woman that she was, she merely smiled and walked away. From that moment on, when the two of us discussed being big Black women, we referred to ourselves and others as Fried Chicken, Watermelon Women.

We laughed at this because that man meant it as a compliment. Fried chicken watermelon women are known for their cooking skills, their mothering skills, their common sense and their strength. She was a feminist before anyone ever invented the word.

My friend, Carolyn tells a similar story about going to a karaoke bar. She was there with several of her large friends. When they got up to do a song, all the White folks sat up, ready to enjoy the show they were about to witness because they just knew these women could blow. Carolyn said she even heard a comment or two to that effect. You see fried chicken watermelon women have got to know how to sing. Folks have been watching Aretha do it for years. Unfortunately, my dear friend and her friends can't sing a lick. The crowd found that out fairly quickly and that stereotype bit the dust.

We all know these women. Some of us are these women. Many of them are in your family as well as my own. These are the big boned, big hipped, big breasted, big bellied women of indiscriminate height and weight who often have several children behind them yelling "Mama" or "Big Mama" or "Ma dear." Friday night you can find the young fried chicken watermelon women in a club with her skinny friends who brought her along to hold the purses. But as Chris Rock notes in his comedy act, she knows she is the sexiest thing walking. She has her hair done, her sharp black dress on wearing an ankle bracelet holding on for dear life. She has on those pumps with the pump fat that looks like bread baking in her shoes. She looks over the strutting cocks that we refer to as men and thinks to herself "Yea, I got a gut but there is damn fine stuff under this gut."

This is the woman comedian Gary Owens refers to as Sister Johnson in the Black church. When asked who invited this pale, White man to the church, he merely answers "Sister Johnson." Every Black church has a Sister Johnson and you can bet she is a fried chicken watermelon woman. If there isn't a Sister Johnson, there is a Mother Johnson. She sits in the third pew to the right wearing her Sunday crown, fanning with the paper church fan mounted on a plywood stick, moaning as the pastor works up steam, yelling a hearty "Amen, go head and preach now, sho nuff."

We know these women as the blessings they are and not the stereotype that has followed them from the days of Gone with the Wind where Mammy reigned supreme.

When Eyvonne and I worked at IBM, we got an earful and an eyeful on fried chicken watermelon women. IBM must have a factory where they roll out pretty little light skinned Black women especially in the positions where clients are involved. Eyvonne, me and others like us were relegated to being administrative assistants because we went about our work unseen and unheard. We ordered and set up food, we made hotel and airline arrangements. We put together power point presentations. We typed reports and checked expenses. We did mailings, filed reports and answered the phone. But we did not appear in public except to clear tables, fetch coffee and deliver paper.

Imagine the surprise when they found out Eyvonne actually had a degree in business. Imagine the shock when they read an article of mine in the Tribune. You could have bought them cheap. All of a sudden we were recognized as worthwhile human beings. Although this realization didn't change either our work status or our income, it did fill us with a sense of pride. For the first time at IBM, we were recognized for our brains and not what we brought to lunch.

For me, this was a turning point. I begin to shop for things at Victoria's Secret and Frederick's of Hollywood. I own bustiers, a leather bra and some absolutely hoochie mama items I would never thought possible before. I began to strut my stuff and this new found confidence had Hispanic men yelling "Hey Mommy" as I walked down the street. It had brothers yelling "Damn Girl" and even a White boy or two checked me out on the street.

But this new found confidence was not about how I looked but how I felt. I learned to enjoy being the smartest person in the room sometimes. I learned to not only boldly show my figure but to proudly exhibit my abilities and talents. And I definitely have some to display. I paid mightily for my graduate education and use it to the nth degree. I may not move as fast as the skinnys but the flies still can't catch me.

Being a fried chicken watermelon woman certainly has its perils but it also has its perks. To paraphrase that old commercial, I can bring home the bacon, fry it up in a pan, eat until I'm full and make him glad he's a man. Cause I'm a fried chicken watermelon woman.

Part 1

LIVING COLORED IN A PASTEL WORLD

White Privilege

Try telling the average White person that he or she benefits because of White privilege and listen to the litany of comments denying it. The most common statement I've heard is the "I wasn't born privileged. My family was (whatever) class. We weren't rich." Those of us who understand the true meaning of those two incendiary words just shake our heads and walk away. We realize it is useless trying to explain what White privilege really is to folks who don't want to own up to it. Yet, I'm going to try or at least give you an idea of what it means to me.

Several years ago, former White Sox manager, Ozzie Guillen was in a pissing match with one of the sportswriters of a local newspaper that lasted several days. Under normal circumstances this would not be on my radar. One evening while watching the news, I heard a broadcaster mention that Ozzie's tirades were going to make it difficult for another Hispanic man to have the opportunity of managing a professional baseball team. I was so angry after hearing this I screamed. My husband rushed into the room thinking I'd hurt myself. Once I'd calmed down and told him what made me scream, he began to rant and rave himself.

Why is one person of color always made responsible for everyone else in his race? Why is it that Whites take any opportunity to keep us from getting ahead by using the behavior of one person to condemn us all? Why is it someone White can do something and it is understood that the behavior is by an individual and not an indication of the entire race. After all, the man who shot up the theatre is Denver is an individual. The young man who shot and killed the people at Sandy Hook is an individual. The Oklahoma City bomber was an individual. Not once has anyone said that all young White men are killers or deranged. Why is that same reasoning not accorded to people of color? That's the million dollar question.

The original title of this essay was "Bobby Knight" because he is a perfect example of what I'm referring to. For years, Bobby Knight screamed, cursed, threw things, hit people and acted a natural fool on television, in press conferences and on the floor of the basketball court. He violated any number of collegiate rules and criminal laws (assault and battery immediately come to mind) and yet he has been revered by those in sports. If he were to indulge in that behavior anywhere else other than a basketball court, he would have spent more than a few weeks staring at the bars of a jail cell. Yet I never once, in the many years he coached basketball, heard anyone say that his behavior was going to prevent a White man from coaching college basketball in the future. Bobby Knight's behavior was attributed to one person – Bobby Knight. Why then are people of color held to a different standard? Ozzie Guillen, regardless of how you feel about his statements, represents one person and one person only – Ozzie Guillen. He is not responsible for what anyone else of his ethnicity does nor is their behavior accountable to him. We are individuals like you with warts, foibles, talents and interests and we should be accorded the singular respect that comes with seeing all people as individuals.

This is the luxury of White privilege – the right to be an individual without bringing entire race along for the ride.

Immigrant Nation

Congress is scheduled to vote on an amendment to the immigration bill. I'm hardly in a position to offer sage advice. It would seem that a great many others who are in a similar situation are offering their two cents. So I feel secure in adding mine. My advice about this is simple – leave folks alone and let folks in.

That was quick, wasn't it? Why? You might be asking, should the US let folks in and leave the folks already here alone? Simple answer – we invited folks here. You're probably asking the next question of when we invited folks here. Simple answer again – the lady in the New York harbor invites people here and has been since she was placed in the harbor in October of 1886. Lady Liberty has inspired millions to come to this country declaring:

"Give me your tired, your poor,
Your huddled masses yearning to breathe free,
The wretched refuse of your teeming shore.
Send these, the homeless, tempest-tost to me,
I lift my lamp beside the golden door!"

These words, taken from The New Colossus, a poem written by American poet Emma Lazarus, are engraved on a bronze plaque mounted inside the lower level of the statue. These words have been echoed around the world. These words give hope to people everywhere, people who feel as though they can actually have the life they dream of if they could only have a chance. These words offer people all over that chance. How could we make such an offer and then renege on the promise?

It never ceases to amaze me when I hear some people say "they" should go back to their own country. If that's the case, almost everyone I know should be on a plane or boat going back to their ancestral countries. This country is a country of immigrants. How else can we explain celebrating St. Patrick's Day (Irish) or Oktoberfest (German), Bastille Day (France) or Columbus Day (Italian)? In Chicago, city offices and schools are closed on Pulaski Day (Polish). We spend an inordinate amount of time celebrating holidays that historically celebrate our connection to other countries and we don't give it another thought. Why on earth would we deny others the opportunity to have what we ourselves have benefitted from for decades?

When you think about all those immigrants who came here by boat, what's the harm in allowing people to come to America by land? After all, those Mexicans crossing the border are simply coming back home. They don't have to board a plane or a boat to get here. They walk.

"Coming home?" You ask. Yes, coming home. In the 1800's Mexico extended into many areas that are part of the U.S. including Arizona, New Mexico, Texas, Colorado, Utah, Nevada and parts of Texas and California. Much land was lost as a result of the Mexican-American War (1846-1848). Since that time, the U.S. government has been pushing native Mexicans further and further south and west. The generations that follow have been answering the call to return to the land of their ancestors and stake their claim in land that was lost through no fault of their own.

The other argument I hear often is the infamous "they." You've heard it. They are taking our jobs. They are overrunning the country. They come here and get benefits they don't deserve. They don't pay taxes. They have anchor babies. They should not be allowed to be citizens. They are dirty. They have too many children. They are responsible for us not getting fair wages. They will do anything for money. They, they, they.

I've heard it time and time again. My answer to the "they" is equally simple. So what! If "they" are taking our jobs, "they" are doing the jobs many of us don't want to do. Americans believe they themselves are too good to bus tables in a restaurant. Americans no longer want to work as gardeners or landscapers. Americans will not work as day laborers or work in a sweaty, dank warehouse. But "they" are. Because "they" know what it is like to live without, be without and "they" are willing to work hard and long to make a living.

I can't begin to tell you how often I've heard the "they" argument and then asked the person making the argument if he or she would be willing to work as a bus boy or day laborer. The answer is always an emphatic "hell, no." "Why should I? I'm from here. Why should I work for less money?" Why indeed. Maybe you should work because you need to and pride doesn't get the bills paid. That sense of entitlement means nothing when rent is due or when your children are hungry. It is that sense of entitlement that separates "they" from us. "They" don't have that sense of entitlement. "They" simply know that if they work hard, they will get some measure of reward for their labors and "they" are grateful for that chance. "They" will not do anything to jeopardize that reward and if means outworking you, that's exactly what "they" will do.

There are so many things wrong with this country. Issues our government should concern itself with like the monetary debt we owe to Japan and other countries, wars that are sucking up more and more resources, 50 million people with no healthcare, public schools that are pipelines to prisons, an environment that is being contaminated on a daily basis and crime. Why is our government spending so much time on keeping people out when we invited them in?

Americans have become so entitled and racist and afraid that we've forgotten our greatest strength. It is that influx of people to a country taken away from its native people and opened up to everyone around the world that made this nation great. Have we forgotten that it was immigrants who built this country? Have we forgotten the many cultures that have made us great? Have we forgotten that we export the promise of freedom and liberty around the world and then get angry when someone takes us up on that promise?

Yes, we've conveniently forgotten. We don't have to. July 4th will come again. While watching the parades and enjoying the fireworks, remember what makes this country great. Welcome an immigrant because in a different time and a different place, that immigrant was you.

The Eye of the Beholder

People Magazine publishes a most beautiful people issue annually. The usual suspects are there – Pamela Anderson, Denzel Washington, Angelina Jolie and the usual two Black women, Halle Berry and Beyonce Knowles.

Black women have entered every major area in American society. They have become well-known doctors, lawyers, athletes, actors, astronauts and even captains of industry. Yet Black women have yet to break into what would seemingly be the easiest glass ceiling in the world to break – the most beautiful list. How is it in the land that has given birth to such beautiful Black women as Dorothy Dandridge, Kerry Washington, Angela Bassett, Gloria Foster, Diahann Carroll, Beverly Johnson and Lena Horne, list only two Black women as beautiful?

Greta Garbo, Carole Lombard, Betty Grable, Jane Mansfield, Marilyn Monroe, Twiggy, Pamela Anderson – they're all blond bombshells. And throughout the history of beauty in the United States, being White, blonde and blue-eyed assured a woman of her beauty. What of the women of color, those women who could certainly change their hair color but not the color of their skin? Who considered them beautiful? What of the damage done to the psyche of women who look but never see themselves on the beautiful list? What happens to them?

For years the images of Black women (and Black

people) were almost nonexistent in popular media. Eventually filmmakers like Oscar Micheax began to make race films that were made for Black audiences. In mainstream film, Black women were usually portrayed as mammies, those large, wise Black women beholden to their white masters or employers. The only other roles for Black women, especially pretty Black women, was that of the tragic mulatto. For years, beautiful Black women found themselves in the same old role. It was because Hollywood had no use for beautiful Black women. When Black women were not relegated to playing mulattoes, they were usually given a scene to shine as a singer like Lena Horne did in a number of films. Then Dorothy Dandridge arrived on the scene. Dandridge was a rare talent. She could sing, dance, act and she was lovely. Cast in two mainstream Hollywood movies -Porgy and Bess and Carmen Jones - Dandridge laid to rest the image of the Black woman as simply window dressing in a movie. So talented was she that the Academy of Movie Picture Arts and Sciences nominated her for a Best Actress Award for her riveting portrayal of Carmen Jones. Unfortunately she died before showing the world all her God given talent.

If the image of Black women in cinema was given short shrift that image in the world of print media was nonexistent. The popular magazines of the first half of the 20th century like Look, Life, Time, Newsweek, and Photoplay always found ways to glorify the beauty of White women and the debonair looks of White men. Black people were once again relegated to the background although there was no lack of beauty within the Black community at that time.

It was not until the late 1950's that Hollywood and New York began to notice the smoldering good looks of Eartha Kitt and Diahann Carroll along with handsome leading men like Sidney Portier and Harry Belafonte. It took good looks along with undeniable talent to make Hollywood start to open its mind to the fact that Black people were beautiful in their own right.

Still it wasn't until 1974 that Beverly Johnson paved the way by becoming the first Black woman to appear on the cover of Vogue Magazine. Johnson and Naomi Sims gave Black women and Black girls the image that had been missing for two hundred years.

Since the 1970's Black women have graced the pages of magazines internationally and walked the catwalks in New York and London. Black women as diverse as Oprah Winfrey and Tyra Banks are invited into homes all across America. Kerry Washington, Angela Bassett, Halle Berry and Monique have all made films that made millions of dollars for their studios. Yet, the United States can only agree that two and only two Black women are good enough to be included in their Most Beautiful List. After more than 100 years in the public eye, the damage to young Black girls is still being done.

These messages, unfortunately, are not only reinforced by popular culture but also by public institutions. Recently, an inner-city high school was found to be constructing practices that supported racial hierarchy utilizing dance classes.

It would seem in this particular area, Black women are taking a huge leap backwards. In the past, even without the great number of beautiful women of color commonly seen, women of color and particularly Black women had a great deal of self-confidence. Women in the Black community were acknowledged no matter their size, definitive African features and myriad shades. This view of Black beauty was evident and the real arbiters of beauty in the community, Black men, seemingly agreed. Both Black and Latino men have always been more receptive to larger body types and ethnic features as opposed to their White counterparts. Thus the image of beauty, regardless of what popular culture deemed worthy, was not an image originally shared by communities of color. As the impossible standards of beauty invade our consciousness, we seem to have lost our way.

Those standards set by the media and the fashion industries have not only been detrimental to women of color but Caucasian women as well.

As the image of beauty has changed, so have the methods of achieving said beauty. The diet industry has grown exponentially with the rise of the thin, White ideal. For those girls and women for whom dieting is not enough, starvation or eating disorders have become the norm. It had always been presumed that such methods were solely the province of young, Caucasian women. However studies have shown that these extremely harmful methods of reaching and maintaining those impossible standards have crossed the lines of both color and age.

In a recent survey conducted by the Mariko Morimoto of the University of Georgia and Susan Chang, it was discovered that White women were featured primarily in ads for beauty while models of other races and ethnicities were featured in ads for cars, health aids and travel. This was found to be the case for both Japanese and other global publications. This global phenomenon has become so prevalent in the Asian world that the most requested plastic surgery is the rounding of the eyes. In this age of globalization, racism in the form of the western world notion of beauty, confirms its ugliness once again.

It may be asked if this trend will ever cease. It may be asked if the world will once again recognize beauty in all its incarnations and cease to accept the Western world's notion of beauty. It may be asked if this notion of beauty is really important in light of the societal ills facing the world. The answers are surely as varied as the number of people asking the questions. Yet one fact remains. There will always be a place in the world for beauty. It is beauty that is valued and treasured in art, literature, music and nature. It is beauty that is remembered when people speak of the world. The notion of beauty is a subjective thing. But beauty, in its many forms, is alive and well and residing amongst us all.

Intentional Inequity

A dear friend and mentor of mine mentioned a couple of weeks ago that during the recent recession/depression, all her Black friends have lost their jobs. Each and every one of them is still unemployed. Conversely, only some of her White friends have been downsized but they are all currently employed. I consider this one hell of an observation considering my friend happens to be White. Her reflection begs the obvious question - Is this inequity intentional?

This question, if posed to the average person, would be answered typically on the basis of race. The average White American would say this lack of return to the workforce of Black people comes down to less knowledge of new technologies or that employers are looking for the best candidates and those candidates just happen to be White. One of my favorite answers is that employers are looking for individuals who can obtain and maintain global business relationships. What galls is that global markets are almost entirely made up of people of color. Only in Europe is the average businessperson White.

The average Black American would simply answer that racism is the root cause as to why so many Blacks have been downsized and have not yet rejoined the workforce. Straight answer, no chaser.

I, too, would agree that racism is the cause of why so many formerly employed Black people are still out of work. I happen to be one of them. During the past five years of my unemployment, I have obtained both a BA and an MS from DePaul University. Although I have achieved what employers say they want most in an employee – a combination of education and experience - I still can't get a job. Unfortunately my current status is not the exception to the rule but is seemingly the rule itself.

Earlier this year, I attended a half-day job seminar filled with downsized Black people. Many of them had never been unemployed and were obviously uncomfortable being at the seminar. One lady gave a very painful testimony about her most recent job interview. She had submitted a sterling resume to a business followed up with a productive phone interview. She was invited to have a face to face interview with her phone interviewer who assured her that her qualifications were first rate and that he had no doubt she would be offered the position. The face to face was just a formality. She arrived early for the interview, checked in with the receptionist and eagerly awaited meeting the man she'd spoken to several times. Shortly a White man came into the reception area, had a whispered conversation with the receptionist and left. After several minutes, the receptionist informed the woman that her interviewer had an emergency and would be unable to meet with her. She was asked to call back in a day or two to reschedule. The lady followed up within 48 hours and was told that the criteria for the job had changed and that she was no longer being considered for the job. It was clear to her and everyone in the room that she was not given the interview because the man had no idea she was

Black until she came for the interview. This would be merely sad if it were not such a regular business practice.

It would seem that the US government in the form of punitive small business regulations, corporations and our pathetic public education system has decided that Black people will continue to be the undisputed poverty class. Schools no longer provide an education but instead prepare Black children in droves for the prison industrial complex. Prisons are using first grade test scores to determine who many people will be in prison with the next 15 years. This allows them to figure out how many jails will be necessary in the future. One company in particular, Corrections Corporation of America, manages 45% of all private prison beds in the U.S. According to their 2011 letter to shareholders (this is a publicly traded company) "only the Federal Bureau of Prisons and three states operate a system larger than CCA. At the end of 2011, CCA housed more than 80,000 inmates in 67 facilities." Imagine the great loss of potential.

Corporation and education professionals (not including teachers) are vocal advocates for the charter school system but that system is merely a way to funnel young people into becoming cogs for the business wheel. This is why so many corporations have invested in charter schools but that same investment is not made to the average public school. If an influx of money and interest can fund charter schools, why is this not done on a continuous basis to fund the already existing public school system? What is happening to the funds generated by the many state lotteries that are supposed to support public schools? Why is school funding tied to property taxes? Why are the children who need the most given the least? More importantly, why do we adults continue to elect politicians whose own children do not attend public schools? In Chicago, a Chicago police officer has to live in Chicago. A Chicago firefighter has to live in Chicago. All public officials have to live within the area they serve. Shouldn't their children be attending public schools? I would imagine if this were the case, the school system would drastically change.

Racism by definition is merely the belief that one race is superior to the other. The most damaging part of this definition is the institutional racism that has been created to further this belief. Will we see the end of racism within our lifetime? I don't believe so. This country is as racist now as it has ever been since it was birthed from both racism and violence.

Can we change this? I would hope so. But not until we recognize that all people including Black people and White people are really only one race – human.

Lessons of the Housewives

One of my guilty pleasures is watching The Real Housewives of Atlanta. I know all the arguments surrounding the show. Any incarnation of the housewives panders to the worst in us. The women of Atlanta show Black women in a less than flattering light. It's fluff about women, weaves, wedgies and wars. Still, I enjoy this show although I don't broadcast it. Guess you all know now. Sunday night I sit with a glass of wine and watch what unfolds.

Regardless of how you may feel about the RHOA (and I'm sure there are a lot of opinions), I watch first for the sheer entertainment value. For the first time, television is giving a platform to the type of Black women I know. My friends are not rich, swaddled in designer clothes, driving high class cars, wearing expensive jewelry, swinging their hair and living large. My friends are almost as broke as I am, borrowing from Peter to pay Paul. A treat for us is getting a scoop of ice cream from Oberweis instead of Baskin-Robbins. But the attitude those women and my friends share is right on.

You must be wondering what I find great about this show, other than the finery and disputes. First I like the way they parent. Although the children are obviously pampered, they don't seem to be spoiled. The women who have children are involved in their kid's lives. The kids are well behaved and even when one poses a problem, Mom is true to form as a Black woman by being firm, loving, scolding and encouraging – whatever's necessary at the time. Not one woman claims her children as their best friends. Each one is determined that her child knows who Mama is and what she is about. Mama may be loving and supportive but she is definitely NOT a friend.

These women are built like Black women. Surely you've seen the shows where women look like stick figures but not the RHOA. They have big butts and big thighs. They look like the women I know. Even the housewives who were models are not skin and bones. The wives all seem to be fairly healthy and comfortable in their skin and their bodies. This is a very important message for Black girls and Black women who are struggling with the images they see in today's media.

Each housewife in a relationship has a real relationship. There is no make-believe romance or friendship. When the couples argue, they argue. Relationships ebb and flow which is the true nature of things. No fairy tale, everything is all right all the time type of relationships but real messy, heartbreaking and happy relationships - the way we know real relationships to be.

The RHOA extend moments to their families. Parents, children, baby daddies, siblings, in-laws, aunts and uncles all have a place in the housewives' lives. This is very indicative of Black folk. My husband I daily talk with one family member or another sometimes more than one and more than once a day. There is no such thing as the nuclear family. There is just family.

The final reason I enjoy this show is that each housewife

has achieved a level of success on her own. Almost each of these women started out fairly standard from a working class background. They came from folks who had to work hard for a living. The ladies are all independent working women with active, successful careers. I take pleasure watching the different ventures upon which they embark. I celebrate their successes and empathize when there is failure. They are smart enough to know their strengths and weaknesses. They are confident in their abilities. They are determined in reaching their goals and work hard to do so. They all have multiple enterprises and they all strive for success but accept failure without drama. When I was a girl, I read about successful Black women but rarely saw any reflection of that on television or the movies. Every week, I see Black women being entrepreneurs and businesswomen. It doesn't get any better than that.

There are so few shows that feature Black women. Almost all of them are reality shows. Girlfriends and Living Single are on in syndication. Like the housewives, these women portrayed successful Black women with a wide range of talents. As much as I liked these shows, there was a part of me that realized this was a scripted show. Scripted shows are important in the way people are shown. But it has always been difficult for Hollywood to figure out how to depict them without resorting to stereotypes. Yes, the RHOA act stereotypically in a number of situations but those stereotypes are balanced by what the women represent to the world.

I can't vouch for the reality of everything that goes on with the RHOA. I would guess that some of it is manipulated. I gladly accept this instead of watching the lone Black friend of the White lead who has no life, no family and seemingly knows no other Black people.

So join me on the couch some Sunday evening and watch an episode. Don't forget to bring the wine.

I Love Me Some Black Men

One of the most endearing characters on the 90's television show, Designing Women, was Bernice Clifton played by veteran actress, Alice Ghostly. She was a spicy senior citizen with a special affinity for Anthony Bouvier portrayed by Meshach Taylor, the Black male deliveryman-partner on the show which highlighted the lives of four Southern women in an interior design firm in Atlanta. At any given time, Bernice would break into the song, Black Man with verve although a bit off key. Of course, the ladies tried to shush her so as not to offend Anthony or themselves but Bernice would persist as often as she could.

Bernice may have been singing to that one Black man but I sing it to all my brothers. I will go to my death saying there is nothing, nothing at all like a Black man.

Of course, I'm biased. My father is a Black man as is my husband, brother and son. I've got a bunch of male relatives and a few really great male friends. My dad resembles Sidney Poitier, a man not hard on the eyes. My dad played up this resemblance and wooed more than his share of women. He is a dapper brother, self-confident, gentlemanly, intelligent and well-spoken. In short, all the things women say they want in a man.

My husband, on the other hand, is almost none of those things. I think he's handsome but he doesn't believe it. He is self-confident, intelligent and gentlemanly but his fashion sense has taken a beating over the years. His most endearing quality is that he loves Black women and hates to see a woman in trouble. He carries bags for ladies he sees struggling. He'll mow your lawn, shovel your snow and curse out the no-good man who leaves these kinds of tasks to the womenfolk. He believes women are precious and should be treated with honor and respect. And of course, he loves me with all that is him. Not too shabby.

I've had my share of jerks but mostly I've been blessed to have the men in my life. They have shielded me, protected me, helped me and loved me. I'm always in good hands when I'm with any of them. But that's not the only reason why I love Black men. Brothers just look so damned good!

Yea, I said it. Brothers are fine even the unattractive ones.

I've given this a great deal of thought and I've studied this. One fact remains. You can work with an okay looking brother. Put him in a great pair of jeans and a nicely fitting t-shirt and you have a thing of beauty.

Or that same somewhat dowdy looking brother. Put him a great dark pin-striped suit with a white shirt and patterned tie and I tell you, that brother could make you swoon.

There is nothing that can be done with an average looking White boy. Trust me. I've seen it. There's nothing you can do with a supposedly good looking White boy. Look at like Anger Management's Charlie Sheen, Psych's James Roday, Ashton Kutcher and Justin Timberlake. They'll do but none of them are worth writing home to mother about.

Think about this. We've spent a lifetime looking at White men on television, on the stage and in film. For the most part, many of them look okay. But compare any of these guys to the few Black men on the screen and I think those White guys are lacking. As far I'm concerned that's one of the reasons there's only ever one Black man on a show. Film and TV executives know that one pretty good looking Black man is worth at least four White men. Even when the Black man is one of the lead characters, he's surrounded by White folks as if the man knows nobody else other than the White folks he works with. The only Black folks these characters know are family.

You know what I mean. Look at current crop of television shows: NCIS: LA, Psych, The Exes, Brooklyn Nine-Nine, Chicago Fire, Ironside, Law & Oder: Special Victims Unit, Revolution, Almost Human and The Walking Dead. In each ensemble cast, there are anywhere from four to eight White folks and one Black man. Just goes to show you. Black men are just too powerful, even for TV.

Modern magazines are worse. People Magazine publishes an annual world's sexiest man edition. Out of all the gorgeous brothers, they've only named one, Denzel Washington, as the sexiest man alive.

That list has included Johnny Depp (who always looks like he needs a bath), Matt Damon (cute okay but sexy, not hardly), Jude Law (probably because as Brits go, his teeth are straight), Nick Nolte/Harrison Ford/Pierce Brosnan/Mark Harmon/Bradley Cooper (don't even get me started on those five, and the latest, Adam Levine (give me a break). To give some of these guys their due, some are handsome and some are merely cute but sexy? But sexy? Not on a bet. Sexy is more than just handsome or pretty. Sexy is a certain something you can't quite describe but you know it and more importantly, you feel it. There's the swagger coupled with a wicked smile and the wink. It's that something that would make you drop your drawers in a heartbeat. It's that something that makes you yell "Whip me. Beat me. Make me write bad checks."

Obviously I disagree with People's choices with few exceptions. Channing Tatum has it. Matthew McConaughey has it. George Clooney, Hugh Jackman and even old ass Sean Connery has it. Of course, People was right on the money with Denzel.

But how could they overlook actors Idris Elba, Terrence Howard, Morris Chestnut, Djimon Hounsou, rapper Common, rocker Lenny Kravitz, model Tyson Beckford and all around renaissance man Jamie Foxx. Let's also not forget the athletes like L.A. Dodger Victor Cruz, the N.Y Giants' Matt Kemp and the N.Y Knicks' Tyson Chandler. I could go on and on but I'm about to lose myself in the throes of ecstasy just thinking about these boys.

Next year when People declares its' pick for the world's sexiest man, maybe, just maybe, they'll actually pick a brother. I doubt it but I can dream. On the other hand, do I really want to share this fantasy group with the rest of the world or do I want to continue to clutch them in my lust filled being?

Don't know right now. Just excuse me as I take care of a little something something. You're on your own.

Worthless

It's been decided, again, that a young Black man's life is worthless. The jury returned a "Not guilty" verdict in the trial of George Zimmerman. You may recall that George Zimmerman shot and killed Trayvon Martin. He claimed he shot in self-defense. It was found, however, that Trayvon was armed only with a can of soda and a bag of Skittles, dangerous only if you have diabetes.

Zimmerman called the police upon seeing the young Black man in the gated community he patrolled and was told more than once to stay in the car until backup arrived. Zimmerman chose to ignore the command and decided to approach the teen. The teen, quite rightly, questioned Zimmerman's authority and a fight ensued. Zimmerman then shot the unarmed teen claiming he was in a fight for his life.

This has been debated ad nauseum by the various political pundits, civil rights leaders, police officials, and the general public. Regardless if Zimmerman felt threatened, one fact is abundantly clear. He made a conscious decision to ignore the advice of seasoned police officers and instead targeted a young man he felt did not belong in the gated community in which this tragedy took place. Zimmerman profiled Martin, decided he was the one in charge and then when he realized he could not contain the situation, chose to end the life of someone he had no business bothering in the first place. His racist unwarranted decisions led to the death of a young man, the devastation of a family and another victory for the racist judicial system people of color have had to contend with for centuries.

What does this verdict say to the Black youth, particularly Black males, in America? No matter who you are, no matter what you say or what you do, America will only see a threat to be removed. Young Black men are vermin who must be exterminated. Black men are unworthy of justice. Young Black men are unworthy of life itself.

With all the hoopla that surrounded the election and subsequent re-election of Barack Obama as president, isn't it ironic that in a country that has been trumpeting the supposed end of racism can look a Black family in the eye and proclaim that the elections were all for nothing. Your son's life is worth nothing. And we have the verdict to prove it.

As an empathetic person, I hurt for Trayvon Martin's family. As a spiritual person, I pray for Trayvon's soul for it will never be at peace. As an American, I hope the mockery that was made of justice that day will soon be over although history and the present prison industrial complex system are proving otherwise.

As a Black person in America, I dream of a day when justice is no longer blind to injustice. But as a mother of a young, Black man, I hope to hell I am never in the position Trayvon Martin's mother. Because I would make sure that only hell could hide someone like George Zimmerman from me. And I wouldn't bet the house money on that!

House Negroes vs. Field Negroes

If White folks in power have learned anything from history, they have certainly learned the lesson taught by Willie Lynch from a speech he supposedly delivered in Virginia in 1712. His speech entitled "The Making of a Slave" is as prophetic today as it was over 280 years ago.

Lynch's speech teaches that in order to enslave a man, you need to enslave his mind and his body will follow. This methodology has been proven useful as civil wars have been waged throughout the African continent and continue to this day.

It was used by slave holders who chose lighter skin Blacks as house slaves leaving the darker people to work in the fields. Once the house slaves were told they were better than the field slaves, the master had only to sit back and watch as the rivalry played out.

Liberal White folks love President Obama. This is mainly because he isn't seen as an average Black man. He is a direct descendant of a Kenyan father. I find it amusing that White America would willingly endorse and vote for a man named Barack Obama but would never do so for a man named Lamar Johnson. Once again, the lesson of that old Willie Lynch speech is lurking in the background.

White folks love Africans of the soil and despise Africans of the blood. They believe native born Africans are more industrious and worthy of their time and compassion. Look at the number of Africans who came to

America and were housed in Nebraska or Minnesota or North Dakota. There is even a town in North Carolina that has adopted 45 Liberian orphans. This is a wonderful thing and I'm happy to hear it but would these same folks be willing to adopt 45 Black children? I think not.

Hollywood seems to have set this trend. The latest designer item is not a Hermes scarf or a Louis Vuitton Bag or even a pair of Manolo Blahniks but an African baby. Madonna, Sandra Bullock, Angelina Jolie & Brad Pitt, Steven Spielberg, Connie Britton and Mary-Louise Parker to name a few, have all adopted children from the continent.

Of course, each of these celebrities has stated they adopted these children because they wanted to call attention to the great number of orphaned children in Africa. They point to children orphaned by poverty, the AIDS epidemic and civil war. I applaud their willingness to save a child from an uncertain future. But what about the thousands of Black children orphaned or in foster care here in the US? Are they any less worthy of being saved?

Unfortunately this ridiculous spat serves neither Africans of the blood nor Africans of the soil. What it does is continue the legacy of Lynch's speech and creates slaves across the Diaspora. Instead of working for human rights around the world, we're playing the house negro versus the field negro over and over again. All the while, worldwide corporations headed and run by Whites are making slaves of us. They're raping the continent of all its natural resources in the name of progress and leaving the indigenous people with little if anything to survive. In

America, our civil liberties are being taken away and the justice system is trying desperately to incarcerate any Black man over the age of 12.

Isn't it time we realized that we are seen as victims everywhere in this world. The only way to stop being a victim is to embrace our common ancestry and make the world recognize us as the great people we are.

Don't put it on your to-do list. Don't stick it on a post-it note. Don't put it on your IPad calendar. Do it today. Our future generations are depending on us. Let's not fail them.

Black Enough

Who is giving out the Black enough cards? If I ever find out, I'm going to smack the hell out of 'em.

Allow me to explain. Oprah Winfrey recently interviewed Rev. Al Sharpton. Generally I dislike her interview style but I do like the interviewees. She and Sharpton were discussing the alarming trend of young Black people deciding that one was not Black enough if he spoke properly or that one was acting White if smart and seeking an education. You're not Black enough if your pants aren't around your butt or you're not screeching the latest from Snoop. They wanted to know where this idiotic notion came from. Me, I want to find that bastard and wring his neck.

Scores of Black people struggled and died to make sure future generations could have access to an education. Those folks fought for the right to vote, to end separate but equal and to make it possible to live the American dream.

And now, young Black people are being told they are not Black enough if they choose to honor the sacrifices made by their ancestors.

I'm more than angry. I'm livid.

As many Americans celebrated the 2008 election of Barack Obama, there were others who declared he wasn't Black enough. I grant you that I, too, have my issues with Mr. Obama. But those issues have to do with his cabinet decisions and his policies. As far as his Blackness is concerned, my issues are not with him but with the folks who proclaimed racism is dead.

It is a fact that the overall feeling about Black people is one of distain. After being in this country since its beginning, we're still treated as second class citizens. We've made strides but we've also taken some big steps backwards. Look at all the states clamoring for Stand Your Ground laws after the Zimmerman acquittal. Or look at the decision of the Supreme Court to gut the Voting Rights Act. Look at how many times President Obama has been disrespected. From a congressman shouting "You lie!" during a joint session of Congress to the many drawings of him as a monkey, he has endured a level of disrespect never experienced by any president to date. No other president in history has endured as much as he has and it's simply because he is a Black man. Obviously White folks believe he is more than Black enough.

So who the hell are these folks that are determining who is and who isn't Black enough? Let's find them and expel them for not being Black enough. After all, we are a proud people. Our ancestors discovered mathematics, invented writing, architecture, medicine furniture, and textiles. Our forefathers developed medicines, engineering, religion, philosophy and built the Pyramids. Scholars and scientists now state that Africans were the first builders of civilization and the birthplace of humankind.

Given the discovery that the first human was African, there should be no debate about who is Black enough. We're all Black. Now run and tell that.

The All-American Kid Next Door

From the age of two until five, my son Jeremey was a child model. He didn't get much work and didn't do any broadcast work but he did several print ads including one for Gerber.

When he was five, he decided he didn't want to do it anymore. I was happy to honor that request because it was all a royal pain in the ass. It just wasn't worth taking time from work to drive him to auditions. The people holding the auditions were rude and the process was horrible. I'm glad we had the experience but it was obvious neither of us was cut out for this.

Jeremey was an adorable child with beautiful, big brown eyes and a wonderful smile. He was articulate and smart. Everything a child needs to make it in the business. He was listed with three agencies (you have to have multiple agents to make it in Chicago) and each agent thought he had what it took to make it in the business.

Besides him wanting to discontinue modeling, there was a deeper reason why we left the business. That reason was the racist attitude of the folks heading the selection process.

Jeremey's agents sent his photos to a national disposable diaper company looking for children for a TV commercial. His photos were returned because the agency making the selection stated they were looking for an "All American" child.

My son was born in Chicago, which, if memory serves,

is in the middle of the U.S. So how much more All American did he have to be? Of course, I knew they wanted blonde, blue eyed children. But mothers of blonde, blue eyed children are not the only ones purchasing disposable diapers. I certainly bought them and almost every mother of a small child I knew bought them as well. What was the agency trying to say? We're American enough to buy the diapers but not American enough to represent the diapers? What a crock!

I wrote a piece about this and sent it to the agency and to the industry trade magazine that printed the request. I never received a response from the agency but I at least let them know how I felt and what the message was they were sending.

This nation was built by immigrants after it was taken from the Native Americans. The Europeans, Asians and Africans that constructed this country were as varied as the flowers in the field yet the establishment still insists that real All Americans are blond and blue-eyed. What a disservice that is to the rest of us.

There is yet another myth perpetuated by the media that galls me. It is the proverbial "boy/girl next door." Often we're told that some actor or actress looks like the girl or boy next door. My question is next door to whom? My neighbors do not look like Matt Damon or Sandra Bullock, two actors who are always described as the person next door.

My neighbors look more like Will Smith and Gabrielle Union. Why are neither of them mentioned as the folks next door? Maybe because our doors just don't count.

The Great White Hope...Revisited

Enough! Enough! Enough! I've just seen one more film that was another in a long line of what I call the Great White Hope movies. You know the ones I'm referring to – the movies in which people of color are victims, powerless to stop the ruling White folks from hurting them. In the midst of the misery and injustice, a lone White man comes along to rally and save the helpless people of color while learning about himself and humanity all in the space of two hours.

I can't speak for you but I've had it up to here. Do the producers, writers, actors and directors think that we're so stupid as to believe one White man can save a whole race of people? Do they think people of color are sitting around waiting for a White Moses to save them from his kinsmen? Somebody get a grip, please.

You may be wondering what's the harm in this. Try this. Film is a powerful medium. People all over the world see movies like The Power of One, City of Joy, Rambo 3, Stargate, On Deadly Ground – just to name a few. This trend covers every genre of movies, from action to science fiction.

People of color see these movies and the images of themselves as victims who are powerless to fight back and too stupid to realize they have the ways and means to resist. We are shown that the answer to the problem is another White man sometimes even one of the perpetuators.

Now the folks in Hollywood would have us believe that all they're doing is providing a little entertainment and that the only message they're trying to relay is that we're all brothers and sisters under the skin. I ain't buying it especially when the only movies in recent years to slightly reverse that trend are the Beverly Hill Cop series and the Sister Act films. And in those movies, I find it odd that in cities as populous and ethnic as Detroit and Los Angeles, the heroes only have White friends.

As a staunch defender of the First Amendment, I wouldn't dream of trying to censor the Hollywood movie machine. However I would ask you, the viewing public, to simply think about the way you spend your hard earned money. Hollywood responds to money, not to threats or protests. So let's give them a lesson in the power of economics.

Instead of seeing another Great White Hope movie, check out A Raisin in the Sun or Gandhi. Rent one or both of them and watch how people of color find strength in themselves in spite of the Great White Hope and not because of him.

Say It Loud! I'm Black and I'm Proud

I'm a seasoned, short, overweight, short haired Black woman. That's my description of me and I'm sticking to it. I could lie about my age but why bother. It beats the alternative. I can't do anything about being short except maybe wear those hooker shoes but that's not going to happen. I could change my weight and my hair but I will always be Black. Not African American, mind you but Black. I've always been Black and will be so until the day I die.

Remember not so long ago when people claimed their heritage. People were Italian or Irish or Polish or Mexican. There was never any question about being American. It was a given that you were American either by birth or by law but it was never a question. Now a simple sentence becomes a compound nightmare with Italian-American, Irish-American, etc. Who the hell has time for that? Not me.

No one asked me if I wanted to be described as African American. People have just assumed that it is the correct term and should be applied to me, my family and others. But it does not. Black describes me and mine. It is the term I embrace and use to describe the entire Diaspora. For me, Africans of the blood (which I am) are encompassed in the term Black and binds me to Africans of the soil (native born Africans). I don't really care if my cousin of the blood is from Cuba or England or Liberia.

For me, we are all Black separated only by geography.

The Huffington Post posted a piece by Jesse Washington entitled "Some Blacks Insist: I'm Not African American." In this article, Washington discusses the history of the term 'African American' which was coined by the Rev. Jesse Jackson, Jr. in 1988 just before his second presidential run. He felt the term was a compromise term that referenced some cultural and historical base like the other ethnicities in America.

Some find the term offensive because they feel it is disrespectful to the generations born in America after the end of slavery. They also feel it negates our part in America history. Gibre George, whose Facebook page is called "Don't Call Me African-American" is quoted as saying "We respect our African heritage, but that term is not really us," George said. "We're several generations down the line. If anyone were to ship us back to Africa, we'd be like fish out of water."

It just doesn't sit well with a younger generation of black people," continued George. "Africa was a long time ago. Are we always going to be tethered to Africa? Spiritually I'm American. When the war starts, I'm fighting for America."

I recognize Jackson's desire for us to determine our identity given what we've endured by White America. I understand the necessity of identity for without such, we're lost. I'm well aware I'm of African descent. My passport states I'm American. Everything I know about myself is rooted in my Black ethnicity, my female gender and my American nationality. Nothing can or will change that.

My ethnicity and my nationality are not mutually exclusive. They maintain a very delicate balance every day. I don't have to give up one to embrace the other. They are as much a part of me as the gap between my front teeth or the curl of my hair.

Like almost everyone else in this country, I am a mutt. My paternal ancestry descends from the Balanta tribe of Guinea Bissau. In America, my ancestors added the Cree Indians from the Rocky Mountains to the mix. My paternal grandfathers were born and raised in Louisiana.

My maternal ancestors are from Texas. I have yet to know where my maternal African ancestry is located but I'm searching.

I've embraced the history of my family and the history of Black people in the United States. We are as much a part of this country and it's making as any other. Our rich history has yet to be fully embraced. It would seem our history in the world begins with slavery with no acknowledgement of what Black people have given the world. It is my hope and prayer that will change and only we can make it so.

In the meantime, let me state for the record that I'm unabashedly Black and unashamedly proud to be so.

Part 2

IN CONTROL & OUT OF BOUNDS

Be Afraid. Be Very Afraid.

There is a group of people who are celebrating around the country. My husband, Jerome is one of them. They celebrate because the sermon they have been preaching for years has finally come to light. They are the conspiracy theorists who can point to alleged NSA whistleblower Edward Snowden and declare "I told you so!"

For decades, we've been hearing that the federal government has been spying on us. We know, for example, that the late J. Edgar Hoover, former director of the Federal Bureau of Investigation, kept files on citizens he felt were subversive. It has come to light that he had the single largest collection of pornography in order to blackmail individuals to cease and desist in behavior he felt was detrimental to his agenda. His files on members of the Black Panther Party, Martin Luther King, John and Robert Kennedy to name a few, were legendary. Although Hoover blatantly violated the civil liberties of many American citizens, he can almost be forgiven for his dictatorial, myopic view of the world as he knew it.

Fast forward from the reign of Hoover to the current spate of U.S. intelligence agencies. We have the FBI which is charged with investigating terrorism, civil rights, public corruption, kidnapping and organized crime. And each of us is aware of the infamous FBI's most wanted list – one of the most visible and effective means of law enforcement communication ever.

The Central Intelligence Agency is charged with collecting, analyzing and disseminating foreign intelligence to the president and other government decision makers relating to national security. The CIA is not a law enforcement agency and is not authorized to conduct operations in the U.S. In matters of national security like counterterrorism, the CIA works closely with the FBI.

The Department of Homeland Security, the knee jerk response to the September 11th attacks, is charged with one goal which is to keep America safe. Although the goal is clear and direct, this department has, in just 11 years, become the third largest cabinet department and the single biggest violator of civil liberties in recent history.

The highly secretive National Security Agency (NSA) and its newer arm, the Central Security Service (CSS) are charged with providing services and products to the Department of Defense, the aforementioned intelligence agencies, government agencies, select allies and coalition partners. This was the agency that employed Edward Snowden and this is the agency we should all fear.

Snowden blew the whistle on his bosses at the NSA informing the American people that this agency has been listening in on our phone calls, monitoring our emails and scanning our mail in the name of national security for quite some time. This blatant violation of the Constitution would be funny if it were not so dangerous.

NSA/CSS officials claim this invasion of privacy has allowed them to curtail various terrorist activities and arrest potential terrorists. None of these plots or the possible perpetrators has been seen nor has it been reported that these individuals will be standing trial for these supposed actions. What this tells me and others is this government sanctioned spying on American citizens is another way of weeding out potential activists who would gain a voice in the way this country is governed. When the government has the means, the motive and the opportunity to crush their opponents before the opponents can even get a foot in the door, it is a very viable method of control.

Snowden has brought to light more than the fact that the U.S. government is committing the same abuses it claims were committed by the former Soviet Union and are currently being committed by Communist China is just one of the many ways our government is playing fast and loose with the Constitution under the guise of keeping us safe. Not to mention the fact that our government is being blatantly hypocritical. Their idea of keeping us safe is keeping us ignorant of what they do and how they do it. Keeping us safe, as they define it, is keeping us in fear.

At this juncture, it is not enough to declare Snowden a hero when he is being demonized by our government. It is not enough to hope he finds asylum somewhere and continues to bring NSA abuses to light. It is not enough for us to recognize that our communication have been and continues to be monitored by a government maintaining we are free from oppression. It is not enough to sign the various online petitions exhorting our elected officials to order the NSA to stop spying on American citizens.

It is time for us to say enough is enough. We need to

flood Congress, the president, the attorney general and the directors of each agency and department with calls, emails, letters, tweets, faxes and postcards reminding them of the commitment they made to observe our constitutional rights. We need to remind them that they work for us. We need to let them know that keeping us safe does not mean they have the right to spy on us and we will not allow any of them to work against us in the name of national security.

Edward Snowden sounded the alarm. It is time for us to get up and get to work. If we don't, we will have taken one giant step towards a future none of us wishes for - the future as predicted in George Orwell's prophetic novel *1984*. Then we really <u>will</u> have something to fear.

It's All about Control

In January of 2013 we celebrated the 40th anniversary of one of the most important decisions in American history, the Roe vs. Wade decision. January 22, 1973 the Supreme Court decided that "a right to privacy under the due process clause of the 14th Amendment extended to a woman's decision to have an abortion." What this decision means to me is that the right to control my body is my own.

I'm sure some of you ladies are thinking that of course, the right to control your body is your own. Why wouldn't it be? Men, of course, never think about this. They never have to. This is about controlling women.

The control of women is not only relegated to control of the body. It is also control of education, economics, legal and political systems in regards to women. So let's just take a moment and go over these issues of control.

Since the beginning of recorded history, every aspect of being a woman has been controlled by men. If you believe the words of the Bible, the first sin was committed by a feeble minded woman. Since then, it has been assumed that women needed controlling. Continuing that biblical theme, people were conceived by men. Going through the book of Genesis, there are chapters upon chapter of who begat whom. None of those myriad of names listed were women. I grant you that it is the chromosomes in sperm that determine the sex of a child but the child must be birthed by a woman.

Moving further through the Bible, women were the downfall of men. David, Moses' sons, Samson – the list goes on. There are verses that have been interpreted as telling women how to submit to their husbands, what to wear and how to behave. There are very few interpretations specifically pertaining to men.

For centuries women were not allowed to own property except by virtue of marriage. Daughters were allotted less land than sons if the father died and the daughter was unmarried. Often the daughter's share of land was given over to the son for safekeeping. In some countries, women are still not allowed to own property or have money. If a wife works outside the home, her wages are the property of the husband. Wives and children are at the mercy of the husband and his family. If the husband dies, his wife can be cast out and the children become the property of his family.

Education of women in the early history of the United States was relegated to reading and learning how to tend to a home. It was thought unnecessary to give a woman access to a high school or college education except as a valuable lesson in obtaining a husband. This is still the case in many countries. Recently in Pakistan a teenage girl was shot in the head for trying to attend school. Still there is hope.

In the West African countries of Ghana, Benin and Togo, billboards dot the land encouraging people to educate their daughters. We can only hope this trend will continue to thrive.

Women gained the right to vote here in 1920 after years of protest. New Zealand gave women the right to vote in 1893 and Kuwait as late as 2005. Saudi Arabia still does not allow women to vote although this is scheduled to change in 2015. We can only hope the ruling family does not change its mind.

Although women lead several Fortune 500 companies, many women's lives and wellbeing is dependent upon a man. As late as the 1970's, women were not allowed to have bank accounts. One of the many enlightening episodes of the television show "All in the Family" shows a frustrated Edith Bunker attempting to establish an account on her own. She eventually finds the courage to inform the banker that she is as deserving of respect and service as her husband. Because of those sexist attitudes, many women found themselves homeless after the death of or divorce from a husband.

This brings us back to control of one's body. Prior to the mid-1970's marital rape was not a crime in the United States. Not until 1993 did all 50 states make marital rape a crime. As with many of the issues mentioned, there are many countries where marital rape is still legal.

This violation of basic human rights extends to issues of domestic violence as well. In the U.S., men who routinely beat their wives were walked around the block to cool off while the wife was advised against pressing charges even as she bled. It was determined better for a woman to have a beating husband than a cheating husband. The financial wellbeing of her family was tied to a violent man regardless of the emotional, mental and physical costs.

Women were told satisfying their husbands' desires was their duty no matter what. Submission in every way was the spoken law of the land. In other countries, women cannot bring domestic violence charges against their husbands because women are first and foremost the property of her husband.

We have all become aware of the issues of honor killings in some countries. The use of rape as instrument of war is widely known and has finally been recognized by the United Nations as such.

As we women in the U.S. breathe a sigh of relief that the we do not have to fear for our lives if we attend school, commit adultery or refuse our husbands, there is still much to be done to obtain and maintain control of our bodies.

Topless beaches are only declared topless if women go without tops. Men do it all the time. I don't know about you but I don't find every topless male appealing yet that male can go topless without breaking the law. Movies are rated X only if there is full frontal male nudity for any length of time. Women, on the other hand, can walk, talk and do any number of things in the nude and the film is only rated R. A telling example of this is Robert Altman's film "Short Cuts." Julianne Moore has a five minute conversation with Matthew Modine baring her genitals for the entire conversation as she calmly irons her skirt. Can you imagine the uproar had that been the reverse?

As someone who is against the death penalty, against the current wars in Iraq and Afghanistan and believes in true gun control (the removal of all guns from everyone including the police), I am stridently pro-choice. Some of you may find that contradictory but I don't. I'm not in favor of late term abortions except in cases where the mother is in danger. But, I don't believe any woman should have to endure a pregnancy because others believe she should.

I have the right to control with whom I share my time. I have the right to determine how I want to be educated. I have the right to speak, own property, control my finances and cast a vote. And I will fight to the death to keep control of my body.

If you don't believe that, try me.

The Terminator and the World to Come

Think about this for a moment. The Terminator was a film about the future of mankind in a world dominated by technology. Remember how desolate the world looked as Reese described it to Sarah Connor. It looked like every picture I've ever seen of Europe during WWII.

Am I saying this is what is to come in the future if technology is allowed to continue unchecked? No, I'm not. I do believe it is a possible future if we continue to eschew what makes life worth living.

I'm not advocating getting rid of technology. That would be impossible to do. I don't want to go back to horse and buggies. Cars are wonderful. Accessing volumes of information in my home is a great luxury although there is still nothing like wandering the library.

Danger is already running amok in our technological world. Our children are becoming overweight at earlier ages because their time is spent texting and twiddling video games instead of playing outdoors. Consumption of mass quantities of junk food seem to be the norm as fruits and vegetables are harder to find and expensive to boot. Going to McDonald's used to be a monthly treat. Now it has become a daily occurrence.

Many children are unable to tell time on an analog clock having only been exposed to digital. They access Facebook, Twitter and countless other social media sites but can't find their home states on a map. Forget about finding another country. Our children have more access to information than at any other time in history yet they are getting dumber and dumber by the day.

Adults are suffering with countless forms of cancer and diabetes is affecting people in great numbers because of lack of sleep, exercise and poor eating habits. People knew directions and could read a map. Now everyone is dependent on a GPS system. God forbid it ever steers you wrong.

Families are strewn across the country with little time to get together. Multigenerational family gatherings are a quaint memory. Socializing with friends is limited to texting, Skype and emails. And getting to know your neighbors is met with derision.

If this sounds like a doomsday prediction, so be it. I see it as a warning and an invitation. The warning is that we can continue to allow technological advances to take over our lives to our detriment. Or we can use technology as the tool it was meant to be and behave civilly and socially as we are meant.

It is our choice. Choose wisely.

Let's Chat about Church

Not too long ago, we had visitors in our home from a neighborhood congregation. They have actually been visiting on a regular basis to meet with Jerome and Jeremey. I am usually on my way out so the most I have time to do is say hello and goodbye in the same breath.

This particular afternoon, however, I was home and able to actually sit in on the discussion. We had a lively debate about a number of issues. One of the most heated discussions centered on church.

The word "church" to me always signifies the people and not the edifice. Upon checking the dictionary, the building is always listed as the first definition followed by the clergy and then the congregants. There are a number of passages in the Bible that mention church and congregation but none of these references pertain to a particular building. They refer to a gathering of people. The Bible says "where two or three are gathered in my name, that's where my church shall be." Using that methodology, church can be anywhere - a home, a club, a hall or a sanctuary. It's not the building that makes the church, it's the people gathered there.

For several years, I worked at the headquarter office of a Christian denomination. People were always shocked when the powers that be did something that was blatantly unfair. They would exclaim 'How could they do that? This is the church!" My response was always the same -

this is not the church. This is the headquarter office. Many people found it hard to reconcile the headquarter office with the church. They assumed the two were synonymous. But they are not. There was and continues to be very little God in that building.

So what is the church, you may be wondering, if it's not the headquarter office or the district office or the building where worship takes place each week? The answer is you. You are the church. It doesn't matter if it's a church or temple or mosque or synagogue or ashram. You are the church. In the end, you are not only the church but you are also the ultimate reflection of God no matter the path you choose.

It's easy to disregard the church if you think of it as a building of worship. It's easy to point a finger and judge when you think of the church as it or them or they. It's not so easy to ignore if the words used are we or us or ours.

We ask why isn't the church saying something about global issues. It doesn't speak out because we don't. Why isn't the church seeking a solution to homelessness or poverty or healthcare or AIDS? It isn't because we're not seeking a solution. Since we are the church, the church can't do what we don't. If we take two steps forward, the church does too. If we take three steps back, the church does as well. To add insult to injury, when a church leader does speak out against an injustice, that cleric is chastised for not focusing on people's souls. It is illogical to think a hungry person can focus on feeding his soul when his daily struggle is feeding his body. The body, mind and spirit are inextricably linked and one cannot be fed if the others are starving. Why would we expect the church to recognize the hunger of one and not the other?

In the end, it doesn't really matter where you worship. You can pray or praise anywhere you feel the desire. If you do so among a group of two or more, you're having church. Don't dissuade yourself from having church if the need is there. You may never know who might need church at that moment. Remember it is not they or them who make up the church. It is us. We have always been and will always be the church. To borrow from Webster, we are "the total complex of relation between people and society." The church goes as we go for we are the church politic.

Happy Devil's Day!

Halloween is my favorite holiday. I remember those days fondly when all I needed for a costume was a pair of baggy pants, an old jacket, dirty gym shoes, some eyebrow pencil smeared on the cheeks and a paper bag for treats. Most of the kids in my neighborhood wore some variation of this outfit. We also had something else in common - camaraderie. We were out and about, ringing doorbells, shouting "Trick or Treat" and getting loads of candy. We even went in to the bar on the corner (this was the only time we could) and received treats from the bartender and money from the patrons.

The adults feigned shock and awe at the little homemade costumes we wore with pride. They pretended not to know us and along with our candy gave each of us "a little something extra" like a nickel or a dime. We swapped candy with each other as we ran from house to house. At the end of the night, we all went home happy, bags spilling over with our bounty and watched as our parents emptied said bounty on the table, picking out their favorites and throwing the unwrapped candy in the garbage. Such was Halloween then.

Since that time Halloween has gotten a bad rap. Tales of horror and mayhem abound. Those tales of horror are not stories of teens throwing eggs or slashing tires just for sport. They're not the stories of the apple with the razor blade hidden inside. It's the story of how those of us who deign to celebrate Halloween are going to be cursed for all time because Halloween has become Devil's Day.

Like me, you're probably checking your calendar and looking for Devil's Day. Let me save you the trouble. It isn't there. So who declared Halloween the Devil's Day? Why, well-meaning Christians, of course.

Now you're really shaking your head. I did too when I first heard this. One year as I was planning to shop for a costume for my son, I mentioned the shopping trip to a friend. She looked at me aghast and uttered "How could you celebrate Halloween? That's the Devil's Day." I thought she was joking but quickly realized she wasn't. She was serious. I asked her why on earth, as a practicing Christian, would she give the Devil a day. She looked at me as if I had lost all good sense and said that dressing in costume especially as a devil or one of his minions and uttering 'trick or treat' was worshiping the devil. I shook my head and walked away. I didn't get it then and I don't get it now.

Here's a very brief history of Halloween. The day has both Celtic and European roots and was originally a celebration that marked the end of summer and the harvest season called Samhain. In the seventh century, Pope Boniface IV declared November 1st All Saints Day to honor saints and martyrs and changed what was once a secular holiday into a Christian one. October 31st was declared as All Hallows Eve which was shorted to Halloween. When immigrants came to America from Europe, they brought their Halloween customs with them. In time Halloween developed not into a secular but a community centered holiday. Today, Halloween generates over $5 billion annually in the U.S. alone. We Americans love Halloween.

Over the past 10 or so years, I've heard a number of people declare Halloween the Devil's Day and have kept their children from participating in the festivities. And my question is always the same - why give the devil a day? Is the devil more worthy of a day than Mussolini or Eichmann or George Wallace or Idi Amin? Each of these persons has done a great many despicable things to humankind. Have you ever once considered having a party or dressing up for Stalin Day? I think not.

It would certainly help if these folks took a minute from condemning others to hell to study a little history. Often it is those who know just a little to take things out of context. Possibly this tirade about Halloween is about control. One of the best ways to control something is to introduce an element of evil. Cigarette smoking was one of ways cool people were able to show their coolness. Now smoking has been relegated to something akin to having leprosy.

I believe those people who declare Halloween the Devil's Day are not trying to be hurtful to their children. I think they honestly believe the rhetoric about Halloween although they don't complain about Santa. I think they believe criticizing the government is treason regardless of wrongs the government may do in our name. I think they believe drinking any form of liquor is against God although Jesus being the party animal that he was certainly didn't think so. His first miracle was turning water into wine so the party could continue. I think they believe it's wrong to have an abortion but okay to execute a criminal because they can distinguish good killing from bad. I think they believe their way is the only way, the right way without giving any credence to the billions of people who may believe otherwise.

It's a good thing that all who believe in God do not have the power of God. Too many people would be condemned to hell and humankind has devised so many ways to hurry and get us there. It's a good thing that so many believe in the notion of a kind, loving God regardless of whether God is proclaimed he or she or is called Yahweh, Allah, Jehovah, Krishna or Satnam. What matters is that God loves us all in spite of our foolishness and believes that life should be lived well. So if that means dressing up as a pirate or princess or clown or even a little devil, sticking up your neighbors for a chocolate bar while yelling "Trick of Treat," so be it.

Now if you will excuse me, I need a nap. I just ate my body's weight in chocolate because we had left over candy from Hallo, oh excuse me, Devil's Day.

Paying the Cost to be the Boss

Famed bluesman B.B. King sings "You got to pay the cost to be the boss." That's a phrase we should all be singing during this time of economic struggle. Americans are paying the cost yet allowing others to be the boss. Something is wrong with that picture.

Have any of you ever worked a job and had the ability to determine how much you were going to get paid, gave yourself a raise of how much you wanted and when you wanted it? Have any of you decided what your benefits were going to be and how long you were going to receive them? I would bet the house note the answer is no. Because you were not the boss.

This is exactly what the members of Congress do. They determine their own benefits and how long those benefits will last. They set their salaries. They determine when and how much their raise is going to be. We give them jobs and we have the power to take those jobs away. We, and not them, are the boss.

So why do we allow this?

The 27th Amendment to the Constitution, ratified in 1992, states "No law, varying the compensation for the services of the Senators and Representatives, shall take effect, until an election of Representatives shall have intervened."

In other words, Congress can't give itself a raise until the next set of terms of office for representatives. This means Congress is allowed to grant itself a raise every two years. The salary for the current members is $174,000 per year.

The Constitution mandates that Congress convene at least once a year. Ordinarily, Congress convenes two sessions a year. The House averages142 days a session. The Senate averages 162 days. This is not to say our officials are not working when not in session. They could be holding hearings, meeting with constituents, traveling on official business or on vacation. At that rate, a member of Congress averages about $1225.35 a day. Nice job, if you can get it.

According to the Social Security Administration, the average person works approximately 238 days a year. The average salary is $44,321.67. So a member of Congress makes almost four times the average American but is in session 96 fewer days.

The president's salary is set by Congress and per the Constitution, cannot be raised or reduced during his current term of office. Currently the president's salary is $400,000 with an annual expense account of $50,000. We should remember that unlike our national representatives, the president has a 24/7 job. He's on call even when he's on vacation. He can be contacted at any moment should a disaster arise anywhere in the nation or the world.

His salary amounts to $1095.89 a day. Not much for the most powerful man in the world who is only allowed a raise once (if he gets elected to another term). Being a member of Congress is a better deal in the long run.

Given the current state of our economy and the growing

financial gap between the rich and poor, it's about time we put our big girl panties on and declare war on Congress. It's time we remembered who is the boss and remind those folks on the hill that we have the power.

Of course, in order be effective, we all have to do it. We can't rely on a vocal minority unafraid to take on Congress. It has to be a concerted effort. It has to be consistent and committed. It will be a struggle because those men and women won't give up or give in without a bloody battle.

We have put Congress on notice. Never take the people for granted. You do so at your own risk.

Adding Insult to Injury

Like many Americans, I'm one check away from homeless. And I'm mad as hell about that. Unfortunately all I can do is rant and rave about the situation like other Americans.

I do realize the ways my family and I are blessed. Every month we manage to pay the rent, buy food and pay the various insurances. The electricity and the gas are on. We have a phone and a computer line. We don't have a car note. And the laundry gets done.

We don't live luxuriously but we're doing pretty well. There are many who are not as blessed.

I've worked for several nonprofits and they didn't have to pay into unemployment. At the time, I didn't know that. Like others, I assumed every employer had to pay into unemployment. Imagine my surprise when not once but twice I was informed I had no unemployment benefits when I was downsized. You could have bought me cheap.

Several years ago, I finally worked a job that paid unemployment. I didn't expect that I'd be unemployed again but silly me, it happened again.

There are few more humiliating things than going to the unemployment office. If you've not had this experience, pray that you never have to.

You show your Social Security card to the person at the front. Have mercy if you don't have it. The receptionist asks why you're there. I'm tempted to say "I'm here because I have nowhere better to be" but I don't.

You're given a form to complete asking pretty much the same question. When you fill it out, you drop the form upside down in a bin atop a long desk. Then you sit and wait for your name to be called. This is the real test of your resilience because the waiting is the worst part. You feel humiliated because you're capable of working but have no work.

Everybody sitting in that room is trying to avoid looking sorry by looking at the floor, reading a book or magazine, eating junk food or just staring ahead. You're not allowed to turn on your cell phone so those game players and texters look about ready to die. No one makes eye contact for fear they might be recognized by someone. You wait minute by minute, hour by hour waiting to hear your name called by someone who looks at you like you're bothering the hell out of them.

The case workers act as if you're personally taking their money. If there were no unemployment office, where would they work? Seems that little thought has eluded them. They only see us unfortunate folks waiting for our turns as crap to be treated by a system that treats formerly working folks like crap and allows the employees to do the same.

Once you're called to a desk, the disgruntled case worker has you fill out a few more forms about your work life. The information is entered in a computer and you're sent on your way with a little speech about your determination coming in the mail and when you receive it, you'll find out how much you'll receive and how you're supposed to report in, usually by phone every other week.

Then you are summarily dismissed like a disobedient child from the principal's office.

There is no reason for the process to be so dehumanizing other than to make formerly working folks feel ashamed about being unemployed. There is no reason to make the process so unwieldy and bureaucratic. There is no reason for the case workers to treat you as though you're taking money from them. There is no reason for any of it.

Except to make you feel as badly as you possibly can.

It's a shame that we decry bullying and yet a program that's supposed to help us bullies us as surely as the bully on the playground. I look forward to the day when we collectively kick unemployment's ass. Personally, I'm looking forward to beating the hell out of Case Worker #5329.

Until then, I guess I'll just make my call.

Sex vs. Violence

There is an old joke about God creating sex that goes a little something like this. God had man and woman stretched out, adding nerve endings and other things to the bodies. When he got to the groin area, he added three times as many nerves as on the other parts of the body. St. Peter saw this and said "Hey God. You made a mistake. You added three times as many nerves there as the other parts." God answered "That was no mistake. When they climax, I want them to call my name."

Of course, this joke tells better than it reads. But the fact is that sex is a natural part of the human condition. It is how we perpetuate the species and how we express love. Sex for all animals is as natural as breathing. Yet we treat it as if it were the most heinous activity known to humankind.

Violent movies are made year after year with ratings of PG and PG-13 and there is no public outcry. Some of those same films are deemed masterpieces. Taxi Driver is considered a classic American film. I consider it to be one of Robert DeNiro's best. It is a prime example of realistic violence. It has been shown year after year on television where its impact can be felt by children of all ages in their homes.

Some parents complain or even call for boycotts of these films or shows. When there is a spate of killings in a city, movies and videogames are pointed to as the cause. When some teen or college student shoots up a school, violent movies and television shows take the blame. Supposed experts debate the harm of these films, TV programs and video games. Other experts remind us of the violence that has been with us since recorded history.

There is never any consensus and once attention has shifted to a new issue, these games, films and shows continue business as usual.

On the other hand, films focused on sexual behavior are vilified. They are branded with the alarming NC-17 rating causing movie theaters to hedge the showings of the films. The dreaded X rating is reserved for pornography but those movie makers embrace the rating often ratcheting up the X to XX or XXX.

Still every once in a while, a sexually explicit film breaks through and is acclaimed as great art. Midnight Cowboy directed by John Schlesinger is the only X-rated film to ever win a Best Picture Oscar and acknowledged as one of the greatest American movies of all time.

Bernardo Bertolucci's Last Tango in Paris was another sexually explicit film upheld as great art. This was a film that inspired reviews of disgust and ecstasy. It's rated NC-17 for the explicit sex scenes.

Recently Steve McQueen's Shame about a man with a sex addiction was rated NC-17 but was hailed as one of the best films of 2011.

Still many filmmakers with a potential NC-17 rating will cut just enough of the film to get an R rating. Boogie Nights, directed by Paul Thomas Anderson, was about a group of misfits who happened to work in the porn industry in the 1970's. It barely received an R rating. And let's not forget the controversy surrounding the film Monster's Ball, a film so explicit, many Black actresses turned down the lead role. The film earned great reviews and earned Halle Berry the first Oscar awarded to a Black woman in a lead role.

Is there a reason why we willingly show violent movies to our children as we hide their eyes from sex?

I would offer several reasons for this. First, violence is created for domination. In the kingdom, the male has to fight his way to dominance and then he has to fight to stay there. He gets to eat first and has his choice of mates. He is only dethroned when a younger, stronger male comes along and defeats him, often by mortal wounds but also by shame.

Our supposed less animalistic selves indulge in its own dance of dominance. We often refer to it as "mine is bigger than yours" which dates back to the first time one man noticed his penis was bigger than the others around him. Wars are waged on this premise.

Next, violence is waged when someone decides they want something someone else has. The fighting in the Middle East was about which country was going to take oil from Iran.

Rape is all about control and not at all about sex. It's about taking away a person's sense of self.

Murder is one man wanting control over the life of another. He wants to determine the ultimate fate of another.

In other words, violence is the way humans choose to

play God.

On the other hand, sex is a natural experience that can experienced by yourself or with others. It is one of the most wonderful practices we have as humans and one we share with all the creatures. There are few things as pleasurable or as wonderful.

If we were to open our minds, we would see that sex is another way of playing God. According to the Bible, God handcrafted Adam and Eve. After that, instead of creating more people, God allowed those two to make others with no interference. There is nowhere else in the Bible where God creates people. He lets us have all the enjoyment of creation.

Think about this. When you hit someone or someone hits you, the pain is physical. You may feel humiliated or angry or frustrated but you absolutely feel pain.

Compare that with sex. Not only do you feel pleasure, you feel energized yet relaxed. You feel euphoric and stress melts away. Orgasms are heart healthy and contribute to our overall wellbeing. What else can give so much in a 30 minute time span?

So am I advocating that you begin inundating your child with porn? Not at all. I realize there is a time for children to be introduced to sex. Each parent has to determine when their child is ready. Instead of dreading the conversation, why not make the talk as enjoyable as the act itself?

Forget the myriad of dead teenage movies like Nightmare on Elm Street or Jason Returns and watch the bittersweet My Girl, the poetic Princess Bride or the coming of age film Flipped. There is no sex but there is romance kids won't find icky. These films can aid in the sex talk that is sure to come. You can frame the conversation based on the love portrayed in these kid-friendly films.

Of course, you can always choose to watch the decapitations in the 300. It will make for some cozy nights with your kids climbing into bed when you're trying to get your sex on.

I'm just saying.

Part 3

NO ONE GETS OUT ALIVE

Our Children, Our Loss

Since the notorious "not guilty" verdict in the Zimmerman case, many of my friends and I have been discussing what it's like to lose a child. Two of these friends have lost sons so the Trayvon Martin case was particularly painful for them.

I have a teenage son in college. He is still living at home since room and board at his school is ridiculously expensive (that's a topic for another day) so he and I see each other every day. Until Martin's death, I took these short encounters for granted. I'm a little uneasy when he is out after dark but I chalk that up to being a protective parent. Now I find I can't go to bed until he's in the house. When I hear that key in the lock, I breathe a sigh of relief and say a silent prayer to the Creator for bringing my son safely home.

I remember the day he was born as if it were yesterday. Hell, I remember the day I found out I was pregnant. I was never supposed to have children. My gynecologist said I would have to go the in-vitro route. At the time, I was married to husband #2 and we were content knowing there were no children in our future. Little did I know we would separate and I would become pregnant after the age of 35.

Dr. Smith gave me the urine test and returned to the examining room to tell me I was pregnant. I told him he was kidding. He said "No, you're pregnant." And I replied "no, you're kidding." Exasperated with this back and forth, he held out a little plastic stick and said "See, the stick is blue. You're pregnant." I was so surprised you could have bought me cheap. He gave me the stick and told me to ask my boss if I could go home because I was not ready for the news he'd delivered. He also informed me that I was near the end of my first trimester, that having a baby at my age and with my medical conditions put me on the high risk pregnancy list and to consider whether or not I wanted to continue the pregnancy. He gave me 48 hours to think it over. Absolutely floored, I was on my way back to work and saw my friend (who eventually became my son's godmother). I told her the news. She hugged me and then steered me toward the office.

I had imagined myself as a mother when I was a little girl playing house. Later as the teenage years approached, I realized I wanted a life of excitement and travel. There was no place in that life for children or a husband and I wanted neither. When my doctor delivered that news that day in April 1994, I knew with all the fervor within me that I wanted my child.

My pregnancy was a high risk one. I had to follow a strict diet, removed from my oral medications and had to administer insulin shots. I went to the hospital two days a week for fetal monitoring and other testing the entire pregnancy. And with all that, I loved being pregnant.

My water broke while I was sitting on a bus coming home from work. I endured 17 hours of labor and on a chilly Friday morning in October, my 19 inch, 6 pounds, 3 ounce baby boy was born. It was and still is the happiest day of my life. Never before or since have I experienced such joy nor have I felt so alive. To this day, my "miracle" baby, my son is the great love of my life.

A couple weeks after my son was born, Susan Smith killed her two little boys. At first, she was on the news begging some unknown Black man to bring back her children. Several days later, it was found that she had murdered her sons. For days after that, I could not put my son down. I held him and cried all day. After all the tests, appointments, trials and tribulations I went through to have this child, I couldn't imagine any mother killing her child. That hurt me more than I could imagine. The death of a child is so tragic to me that when I hear about the death of anyone's child, I shed tears.

When mothers get together to discuss husbands, work, the economy and the world at large, we all smile when we talk of our children. We admit that our children can be pains in the ass. They aggravate us. They make us cry. They worry the living hell out of us. We can't wait for them to be on their own and out of our hair. But no matter how stressful they make our lives, we love them fiercely and can't imagine life without them.

This is how the death of Trayvon Martin affects me and my friends, the mothers who meet. Those mothers who've lost their sons can barely find the words to express their sorrow and empathy for what Trayvon's mother is experiencing. For even when they are laughing, there is a just a hint of sadness. The missed birthdays, the many Christmas gifts that will never be exchanged, the Thanksgiving dinners that will never be shared, the wedding that will never happen, the grandchildren that will never be – there is nothing that comes close to that pain. Imagine burying your child when you've been paying insurance premiums so your children can bury you.

I wouldn't ever want to trade places with Martin's mother or my friends who have lost their sons. We all lost a child that night. We've lost many before then and unfortunately, given the way we treat children as afterthoughts instead of people deserving of love and protection, we can expect to lose more. Those deaths will be great losses to the world for those are futures that will never be.

I find myself hurting a little whenever I hear of another child lost to violence no matter where that child may live or who that child might be. All children are our children and as adults, we are responsible for them all. When we fail our children, we have failed as human beings.

Step Away from the Self-Help Aisle and Help Yourself

Have you ever wandered through the self-help aisles in a bookstore? I do every time I visit a bookstore. The number of books claiming to help us find joy, happiness, contentment, creativity, life force and the like is staggering. I never realized how many people out there have given such thought to helping the rest of us live a fulfilled life. It never occurred to me that so many of us were so screwed up that we needed more than 100 other people to help us fix ourselves.

The usual suspects are always there. Tony Robbins, Dr. Phil, Eckhart Tolle, Iyanla Vanzant, Rick Warren and Joel Osteen, to name a few, have at least two books in this category. I find it interesting that almost each of these people is a motivational speaker, a psychologist or a minister. They've all come through some sort of personal crisis and each has come out on the other side with great wisdom to share and great amounts of money earned. Each one is a living encyclopedia of the "get up and get moving" pronouncement. If not that, it's the "get up, get praying and then get moving" declaration.

Don't get me wrong. I know there are millions of people who are in need of guidance. Anti-depressants are being prescribed in record amounts to the young and the old. Suicides are on the rise. Cults are pointing at the changes in nature and proclaiming we are in the last days.

Religious cable channels have tripled within the past 10 years. Plastic surgery and body modification is no longer the exception but the rule as we mold and shape ourselves in an attempt to stay young and lithe. Even the rich and famous seem to be out of control trying to find their way. What the hell is happening to us?

For as long as I can remember there have been self-help books. Napoleon Hill's *Think and Grow Rich*, Dale Carnegie's *How to Win Friends and Influence People*, Dr. Norman Vincent Peale's *The Power of Positive Thinking* and the *Bible* are the books I remember from my youth. Almost every household had at least one of these books on the shelves and they all had Bibles. These were the tomes people turned to when they were depressed or looking for the way to a fulfilled life.

Fast forward to 1987 and Joseph Campbell's *The Power of Myth* opened the flood gates. From there came Stephen Covey's *The 7 Habits of Highly Effective People* and Susan Jeffers' *Feel the Fear and Do It Anyway*. The 1990's introduced Robert Bly's *Iron John*, Anthony Robbins' *The Giant Within*, M. Scott Peck's *The Road Less Traveled*, Richard Carlson's *Don't Sweat the Small Stuff* and Deepak Chopra's *The Seven Spiritual Laws of Success*. According to the Columbus Dispatch in January of 2013, an estimated 2000 self-help books are published annually resulting in a $10 billion a year business. Self-help books sell more generally in January when people are looking to start over in the New Year.

What does this say about us as people? Is it possible that we need guidance from 2000 books to turn our lives around? Have we become so lost that we actually believe our problems, our lives, our successes and our losses can all be corrected or directed by someone who has no knowledge of us personally? Have we strayed so far from our center?

I wish had the answer. I wish I could recommend one of those 2000 books that would answer all those questions. I wish I could tell you why you're here, tell you what you were destined to be or destined to do. But I can't. I can't because I don't know you. And on any given day, I don't even know me.

I'll share with you what I do know. Sometimes asking the questions is enough. Sometimes taking a deep breath is enough. Sometimes crying until you fall asleep is enough. Sometimes giving yourself a hug is enough. Sometimes it's the small things that answer the big questions.

Most importantly, I know what I don't want. That gives me a place to start. Sometimes knowing what you don't want can help lead to what you do want. That may not be the way you would answer life's questions but it's a start. Sometimes a start is all you need.

Let's Talk...To Each Other

This post is going to put me on somebody's shit list. Actually, it's going to put me on a lot of somebody's shit list but that's okay. I can take it.

Recently I attended a day-long conference regarding social justice issues on a global level. Attendees were seated at tables designated by a particular issue. The seven of us at my table were interested in fair labor practices. Three of us were eating our lunch as the other four were either texting or tapping a tablet.

I took a sip of water and then declared to the table, "How about we do what people used to do and talk to each other." After a few uncomfortable seconds, the ladies put their gadgets away and we agreed this would be a good idea. We introduced ourselves and enjoyed a great talk.

Normally I wouldn't do such a thing. But I've really become fed up with this habit we've adopted of being so discourteous as to ignore the people we're with.

How often have you seen two people sitting across from each other in a restaurant and both are talking on the phone? Several years ago, this was something of a shock. Nowadays it seems to be accepted behavior. Is there something wrong with me or has this become the "new normal?" Where was I when it was decided people should go out together but spend time apart talking on cell phones? This has become so regular that people take me to task when I mention it. I guess when people are out together, they mean they are occupying the same space but not interacting with each other. Silly me!

Another example of this egregious behavior occurs on public transportation. Riding public transportation has always been a bit harried. People are mean, pushy and downright discourteous.

Now people insist on sharing their entire conversation with everyone on the bus or the train. Although you could care less about the petulant kids or the stingy boyfriend or the irritating co-worker, you hear the entire conversation. If you look at the person talking, you're given a withering stare and sometimes asked why you're listening in on the conversation. If you answer that the person is talking so loud you can't help but hear, all hell breaks loose and you become part of the messiness you hoped to avoid. There is no way to win.

When did using technology absolve us from practicing common courtesy?

I'm not advocating that we ban the use of technology. I recognize the great advances new technologies have made in our society. People are living longer and better. We make friends all over the world without leaving the comfort of home. We can access all forms of information in a short period of time. Technology has become useful in ways we could only dream about 20 short years ago.

Technology, however, should not absolve us of our basic humanity. Technology is a tool and should be used as judiciously as any other tool. It should not be the end of a civil society.

So I'm asking if it's possible for us to use technology the way it was meant to be used and for us to socialize the way we were meant. Is it possible for us to have a conversation with the person seated across from us instead of the person who is miles away on the other end of the phone? Can we get together for coffee or lunch, not text and give our companions our full attention? Can we ride the bus without making everyone privy to our lives? Can we watch a movie without the proliferation of cell phones going off disturbing the movie experience? Can we sit in a meeting without being interrupted incessantly by phones chirping and chiming?

Is anyone bothered by this continued encroachment upon courtesy and civility? Or is it just me?

50 Shades of Crap

During my recent hospital stay, my brother asked if I'd read *50 Shades of Grey*. "No. You know I don't read romance. Have you?" "Yes, I have and I think you should give it a read. You might find it interesting." This was how I lost four days I will never get back nor will I trust my brother's reading recommendations especially when he says I might find it interesting.

I started the book on a Wednesday afternoon and I can recount what was worse during my stay. Of the hospital bed, the endless bloodletting and the hospital food, the reading of *50 Shades of Grey* was hands down the worst.

For those of you unaware, this book details a woman's coming of age with a rich man who is addicted to bondage and domination. I have nothing against bondage, domination and submission. I've dabbled a bit myself. My problem is someone with very little talent becoming a cultural icon in the literary world and a symbol of women's liberation. I've grown accustomed to untalented people making waves in the worlds of music, television and movies. However it pains me when this happens with books. It's like mixing Kool-Aid with champagne.

The reason this book caused such a stir is because the subjects of bondage, domination and sex are generally written by men with very little regard for the women except as vessels for semen. The idea that a woman would write a book with graphic sex scenes not dripping with romance seems to have come as quite a shock. This book with its mature subject matter made all the "legitimate" bestseller lists.

I came of age when the women's movement was gaining widespread support and visibility. Women were burning bras, marching against pornography shops in Times Square, demonizing Hugh Hefner and debating the legalization of abortion. That's why I'm finding it so hard to understand why *50 Shades* is such a phenomenon. Has no one read Xaviera Hollander's *The Happy Hooker* or saw the movie? Did everyone miss Erica Jong's *Fear of Flying*? Has anyone read Pauline Reage's *The Story of O* which explored similar subjects? These books were radical for their time because most people never seemed or wouldn't admit to the fact that women enjoyed sex in all its incarnations and that women actually wrote these books. People act as if *50 Shades* was the first novel to delve into one of the lesser discussed areas of sexuality when in actuality it is following a trail that has already been blazed.

None of the books I referenced are great literature. They will never replace D.H. Lawrence's *Women in Love* or James Baldwin's *Another Country* or any other great work that explores sexual morays. What these books do is ask us to question how far are we willing to explore for pleasure, if pleasure and pain are co-dependent and what is normal. I claim no answers to those questions. I believe no one does and if someone says he does, he also has a bridge for sale.

I can answer that we all ask these questions and the answers are as varied as the people who ask. There is no wrong or right. There just is. Maybe that was the whole point of *50 Shades*. A good idea poorly executed.

I might just send my tattered copy of *The Story of O* to E.L. James. If she's going to write about submission, it's best to submit to a master. Or get your butt whipped in the process.

Public Transportation

I love public transportation! There, my secret is out. My mom says I would ride the bus to China if I could and she's right. I've ridden public transportation in cities across the U.S. and other countries. In Chicago, I sit in my favorite seat when I can and I read. I don't have to battle with traffic jams, the endless stopping and starting. No traffic signals, honking horns, slow walking people or crazy driving cabbies. I can rest, relax and leave the driving to someone else. It doesn't get any better than that.

On the other hand, I can't stand many of the riders. If you ride public transportation as much as I do, you'll recognize these people and why they bug the living hell out of me. There are rules of courtesy that all who ride public transportation should adhere to and if you can't abide the rules, then don't get on the bus.

First there are the hustlers. Now I respect anyone who hustles for a buck. I just don't want to be hustled. Riding the bus or the train is restful and relaxing for me and I don't want to be jarred out of my peace by a group of rappers or someone selling a chapbook or begging for a church or preaching. It's much too much in the morning and irritating as hell at the end of a long day.

The loud talkers are next. You know the ones. Everybody has to be privy to their business. You don't mean to be but they're so loud, you can't help but hear. That also goes for those folks on cell phones. Trains are noisy and no one can carry on a decent phone conversation while riding the train so don't do it. Wait until you can hear and speak without yelling at the top of your lungs.

I can't stand people with too much luggage or stuff blocking the aisles. Buses in Chicago have an area for passengers in wheelchairs, walkers and strollers. The seats lift and the wheelchairs or strollers lock into place. Use the seats! Don't sit on the seat and put the walker or stroller in the middle of the aisle while people attempt to squeeze by. It's rude and it's stupid. If you have too much stuff to carry and place on your lap on the bus, get a ride, get a cab or call a friend.

The same goes for those with so much luggage, they take up seats on the train. I realize taking public transportation to the airport is cost effective but if you have that much luggage, you need to travel in private. And I will not stand up so your luggage can sit. Deal with it.

Finally, you folks with backpacks. Take them off. It's almost impossible to walk down the aisle when multiple people are all wearing backpacks. I take mine off before I get on the bus or train so others will be able to board. It's only courteous to do so.

This also goes for the folks who stand in the front of the bus. Segregation is over and everyone can ride in the front or the back of the bus. Standing at the front of the bus blocking others from getting on or off is not only discourteous, it's stupid. Very few blind people ride public transportation so we can all see you. If your need to be seen is that bad, find a shrink and have a long chat about self-esteem. And if you are standing by the driver due to fear, let it go. If something breaks out on the bus, the driver will not protect you. It's every man for himself at that point.

Speaking of courtesy, my final rant is for those folks who seem to think they are at home when sitting on the bus. The man sitting next to you, spreading his legs like he is the answer to John Holmes (The late Holmes was a very well-endowed porn star.) If a man is packing that much, he has obviously missed his calling. There is a stage in Vegas with horny screaming women waiting for him.

The women are just as bad. They cross their legs in the aisle like they're sitting on Letterman's couch. When you bump up against their foot, they give you a look as if you were the jerk. I simply say "Move your foot. This is public space." and push my way through. Public transportation is not the place to be seductive. Do it at the right time and the right space. If you can't catch someone someplace where people are out to be caught, maybe you need to change your bait.

Marriage Ain't for the Faint of Heart

Illinois is the 16th state to make same sex marriage legal. It is a great step forward in recognizing LGBT couples as legitimate. Hopefully this will become the law in all 50 states.

The signing of this law caused me to wonder about marriage in all its complexities. Marriage is a government endorsed contract combining two individuals into one entity. Religious denominations see marriage as a God ordained combining of two individuals into one. Marriage is the government or religious equivalent of hydrogen and oxygen making water.

There is nothing inherently wrong with marriage. Some people do it once and manage to make it last until the proverbial death do they part. Other like me, do it more than once and hope to can get it right. Still others see no reason for it and decline to participate in this centuries old institution.

Whatever your feelings about marriage, I think one thing is abundantly clear. Marriage is difficult. It takes commitment and hard work. It can be joyous or torturous. More importantly, there is no right or wrong way to do marriage. Like fingerprints, marriages are as varied as the folks in them.

Given this new entry into marriage laws, I'd like to see another change pertaining to marriage. That change is to make marriage renewable. Radical idea but I know people who agree.

I've often heard marriage compared to parenthood. Nothing could be further from the truth. As a parent, one is legally, morally and ethically bound to care for a child. But when that child reaches either 18 or 21, that obligation ends. You'll always be a parent. But you are no longer bound to that child and there are no legalities tying you to that child.

Think about it. With the exception of parenthood, there is nothing in life that is permanent or ties one to anything other than marriage. We vow "till death do us part."

Once that contract is signed, you are bound to another as if you were bound to your child. Unlike parenthood, the only way to unbind yourself from a spouse is to file papers and appear in court where the government ends the contract.

So if a marriage can be contracted, shouldn't it be renewable?

If marriage were renewable, say every five years, you and your spouse could decide if you wanted to continue or let the marriage go. If you don't renew the marriage, you would be able to go your separate ways without the emotional roller coaster of an unplanned divorce.

The time has come for us to consider this. Imagine being legally able to end an untenable situation with no muss or fuss. Those individuals who want out to see what's out there without fear of reprisal. It may help women end abusive situations. There would be no need for divorce because all the legalities would be handled at the beginning. Parents who chose not to renew their license with each other would still be responsible for their children but the children would benefit from the peace a dissolved marriage could bring.

What brought this to mind originally was that I had been unable to remain married after the five year mark. You've heard of the 7 Year Itch but I have the 5 Year Phobia. After five years, I would begin to reconsider my marriage and it always came up short.

This time around, however, my husband and I are actually into the double digits. Friends and family are bewildered but I'm totally amazed to be in a marriage that has lasted more than five years. The five year mark came and went and there was little, if any doubt that I would remain in this for the foreseeable future. And it seems to be as strong now as it was when we first embarked on this journey. Either miracles do happen or maybe I'm just too tired to care.

Regardless, in this age of instant gratification, surgeries that reconstruct entire bodies and technology so far advanced that Star Trek and Star Wars seem outdated by comparison, why are we holding on to the antiquated notion of promising commitment until death? Could it be there is something comforting in the belief that we will go into old age with a life partner? Could it be that marriage is more than a government or religious binding contract? Or are we're just too lazy to deal with something else that might have to be renewed?

I like the idea of renewing your marriage. I also like the idea of growing old with someone who knows me well and wants to be with me anyway.

Disney used to rate its rides A-E with E ticket rides being the best and most spectacular. I love the fact that my husband realizes I'm an E ticket ride and he's the only person in my line.

Sports Widow

If my husband ever finds this out, I'm toast. The truth is I really do enjoy sports. Not watching, mind you, but having him devote all his spare time watching them.

There is nothing quite liking watching your partner getting so involved in the game that everyone and everything in life takes a backseat. Jerome gets so engrossed, he curses at the television at the top of his lungs. He jumps up, stomps the floor gesturing wildly while taking the players to task for missing a touchdown or blowing a basket. Watching him is more enjoyable than watching the game.

The real reason why I enjoy sports is that the game gives me the perfect opportunity to do the things inside and outside the house that I enjoy. I use game days to shop for shoes or spend hours at the bookstore. I see that foreign film that he sits through bored asking when it's going to end. I have brunch with friends or visit a bar with a great selection of single malt scotch. I go to a theater matinee or see a dance performance. In short, I have myself a damn good time without having to drag along a complaining husband.

Sports widows are everywhere and the number is growing. Each generation offers up another group of men willing to sit in front of a television eating nachos, drinking until dusk bemoaning the fate of some team somewhere.

If you're not a sports widow, you might be video game

widow. Guys get together playing the latest and interminable X-Box or Nintendo Wii game all the while eating those same nachos and drinking the same beverages.

Since us girls know that our guys are held hostage by the game, why do we spend time begging them to talk to us while the game is on? We want to discuss the children (they're as bad as you think) or whether we've gotten fat (yes, we have). We want to know if he still finds us attractive (Duh! If he didn't, he'd be gone).

Sometime ago, a friend asked me how I dealt with "the game." I told her I loved the game and she should learn to love it too. After giving me one hell of a look, she wondered how I could be content being ignored while the game was playing. Didn't I get mad when my man refuses to talk to me when the game is on?

I took a deep breath and a sip of scotch as I slowly laid some truth on her.

Game day can be either the best or the worst thing that can happen to your relationship. The choice is up to you. You can be a nuisance and try to make that man talk to you when you know his attention is elsewhere or you can leave him the hell alone and let him watch the game in peace.

While he's watching the game, you enjoy a spa day. While he's yelling at some large men knocking the hell out of other large men, you could be shopping without hearing him complaining about the time or the money. While he's watching tall men in shorts bounce a ball, you could be at the movies watching the chick flick that you have to drag him to. While he's watching someone pitch a ball at some guy's head, you can take in a matinee at the theater or the ballet. You could even stay home, give yourself a mani-pedi, take a long hot bath while reading your favorite book and sipping a glass of wine without disturbance. When you think about it, sports widowhood is one of the greatest things ever.

When the games are over (they do eventually end), you and your man have things to share, maintaining your togetherness by having experiences apart. If that isn't good for a relationship, I don't know what is.

On the other hand, you can learn to love football, baseball, basketball and the like. You can learn the game, the rules and the stats. Your man will be happy with your newfound knowledge of his favorite sport. Then he'll start watching the game at the sports bar.

And you're alone again, naturally

My Dilemma

Taking time away from writing gave me a unique opportunity to recognize why this piece has been difficult. You would think having the unique chance to express my thoughts and opinions would be easy but it's not. The reason why it's been hard is because I was having a hard time trying to reconcile the image of the word church.

You're probably wondering what is so difficult about that. We all have a pretty uniform idea of what a church is and what it stands for. In my zeal to be respectful and responsive, I've encountered the same dilemma our country has encountered and that is the attempt to be inclusive, to include the church universal or the church politic. How can I hope to reconcile what we, as a country, have not yet been able to?

There has been an ongoing debate as to whether or not the U.S. is a Christian nation. Anyone who remembers their history knows that one of the tenets upon which this country was founded is the freedom of religion. Though the Constitution outlines the separation of church and state, it's been evident over the centuries that the Christian ethics and values were used as the anchor of government. The president and every holder of political office sworn in does so with a hand on the Bible. Our currency declares openly "In God We Trust." Sessions of Congress open with prayer. There is a weekly prayer breakfast in the capital. The list of Christian ceremony and ritual within the country goes on and on. Because of the right of freedom of religion, we also embrace Judaism, Islam, Buddhism, Hinduism and lesser known religions like Wicca, Druidism, Rastafarian and a whole host of others too numerous to mention. We may not know them, we may not recognize them but we all acknowledge their right to exist here.

I made a difficult decision but one that makes things clear for me. I'm a practicing sort of Christian (more practice than actual achievement) attempting to write sometimes from that perspective.

I'm not abandoning my respect for other religions. In fact, I plan to continue honoring them. And the best way for me to accomplish that goal is to write from the perspective I know. Attempting to be all things to all people means that I would do a disservice to those I mean to honor.

I believe in all paths to God and I have no intention of adding potholes to someone else's path. For me, that is not only the Christian way but the right way.

The Question is Not What Would Jesus Do?

WWJD? How often have you seen this on a bracelet or t-shirt or bumper sticker? I've seen it thousands of times and I wonder why we are asking the question. The questions we need to ask as a society are: Who would Jesus kill? Who would Jesus leave homeless? Who would Jesus let starve? You get the point.

This country considers itself to be a Christian nation. In God We Trust is the motto on our currency. In court, witnesses are asked to swear on a Bible. Yet this Christian nation killed the native people who were here. It grew and prospered on a system of slavery. It usurped land from Mexico and is angry that Mexicans actually want to come back to their original lands. What form of Christianity is this? Certainly not the one we espouse to believe in. History bears out these facts.

It is easy to chastise this country for the ills it has and continues to perpetrate on the world in the name of God. Extremists Muslims kill hundreds of innocent people with bombs in the name of Allah. The U.S. continues to kill hundreds in a war that was based on a lie. Women and children are raped and murdered in the name of Yahweh in Darfur. Do we believe this is what Jesus had in mind when he asked us to love our neighbors as ourselves?

We know the answers to those questions listed above. Jesus would kill no one. Jesus would leave no one homeless or sick or starving. So why are we continually asking WWJD? He would do exactly what we are not. He would speak for those who have no voice. He would let the government know that all life is precious. He would work to make sure everyone had shelter, healthcare and food. He would not rest until all was put right.

We know what Jesus would do. The question to ask is what will you do?

Grandma

My grandmother, Mary Liza Holmes Seavers, was the single biggest female influence in my life. My mother died when I was six. Although I have memories of her, the woman who taught me to be a woman was my grandma.

I was a lucky girl. I grew up in an age where grandmothers were not 40 year old women vying with their 20 year old daughters for the attentions of a man. My grandmother was married to one man for over 30 years and when I arrived on the scene I had the luxury of having both of them in my life until my grandfather died.

Mary worked for over 25 years at Mercy Hospital in Chicago in housekeeping. We've all seen those faceless men and women who came into our hospital rooms to mop, make up beds and empty the trash. They did their job efficiently and quietly and moved on to the next room as quickly as they came into ours.

Every day, she awoke at 5am and quietly went about her morning routine which included combing my hair while drinking her coffee. She left at 6:15am and took three buses to work. She refused to take the train because she didn't trust it. She worked her eight hours, took those same three buses back home, made dinner, washed dishes and prepared to do it all over again the next day.

Like so many women in my Englewood neighborhood, she worked hard. She drank Schlitz beer and smoked Salem cigarettes. She played cards and was a member of a social club that met monthly. They planned club sets at various lounges and divided the proceeds amongst themselves. She disciplined me and the neighborhood kids with a yell and a hard smack on the butt. She also handed out fresh fruit and shared homemade ice cream with my friends. We never once talked back or thought it was odd to be chastised by adults on our block. We were raised by the village on 73rd and Sangamon.

Grandma enjoyed travel although she refused to fly. She and my aunt Mary took Amtrak to New York for the World's Fair. We took Amtrak to Dallas to visit my mother's relatives and took Greyhound to visit her brother, my great-uncle, in Michigan. We took a chartered bus to Indiana to attend the Indiana state fair and my first trip to Great America was a chartered bus trip she planned to St. Louis.

My grandmother took me to the legendary Amphitheater to see the Ice Capades, Ringling Brothers Circus, Peter Pan with Mary Martin and wrestling matches. Before Operation PUSH, there was Operation Breadbasket and we went to the expo every year and saw the blues show. She took me as often and to as many places as she could. We had wonderful times out and about town including riding the bus downtown to visit Sears and Goldblatt's. We took a cable line bus on the westside to visit my great-grandmother. Even riding the bus to the grocery store or making a trip to the bank was adventure.

What I remember most is what she taught me. Girls today don't have any idea what they've missed especially when it comes to the kitchen. Holidays were the best when

Grandma cooked and I was her helper. She did the hard work and my job was to cut the vegetables she put in her dressing and potato salad. I also stirred the sweet potato mixture for her wonderful sweet potato pies. She always let me lick the spoon. To this day, sweet potato pie is my favorite although I have yet to find one as good as hers.

She also taught me to be a lady and a woman. She always stressed to me that there was a time to be a lady, a time to be a woman and a time to be a whore. She told me smart girls are the ones who know when to be what and never get the three confused. I learned to act like a lady whenever I was out, a woman at work or when faced with a problem or an issue, and I learned to be a whore in private with my husband. Today's young women seem to have no idea of when to be what.

As a mother myself, I catch myself moaning about the good old days. Those of us who do this aren't thinking about segregation or the Viet Nam war. We aren't thinking about gang wars and partisan politics. We aren't thinking about the assassinations of the Kennedys, Malcolm X and Martin Luther King. We're thinking about summer nights catching lightening bugs, eating cold watermelon and homemade ice cream. We're thinking about a time when you could play outside through all four seasons without fear. We're thinking about knowing everyone in your neighborhood including the store owners. And we are thinking about the smells and the feel of grandma's house. We remember Grandma, Big Mama and Ma Dear. She remains in my memories and my heart and I am a better person for it.

My Friend, Death

We've all grown up hearing only two things are certain, death and taxes. If you're rich in America, only one of these is true. The other is a non-issue. Obviously I'm speaking of death. Once we're born, every day we live brings us one day closer to death. It's a very sobering thought and one most people avoid. We spend vast amounts of time and money trying to stave off the inevitable. And death IS inevitable. It is the one appointment we can't cancel or reschedule. Death sets its own timetable for each of us. Thus the only thing we control in terms of death is how we meet it and that's only if we have the luxury of knowing when it's coming. If you die in an accident or meet your end in an act of violence, you don't even have the luxury of facing death on your terms.

Why, you may ask, am I writing about death instead of focusing on any myriad of subjects? The short answer is because I want to explore death and time. The real answer is somewhat different. Death scares me and fascinates me. I'm not the only one. Check out almost any Woody Allen movie. He spends a great deal of time on the subject of death. Ask the average person if he is afraid of death and I would bet that person would say yes. However I think what we really fear is not so much death at all but what happens after we die.

The faithful among us believe there is some form of life

after death. We go to heaven or hell or purgatory. That is all predicated on how we live now. Others believe we become part of the cosmos, having no form or shape but constantly moving through the solar system in never-ending time. Some believe we are reincarnated to other forms or people which is once again, predicated upon how we live each previous life because we never cease to exist. Finally there are those who believe death is the end. We return to earth as the dust to be walked upon as the others who have preceded us. Me, I'm not so sure and that uncertainty is what scares me the most. I don't have enough faith in any of these scenarios to give me comfort.

That discomfort is funny given that one of my favorite shows recently aired its series finale and its focus was death. I'm speaking of Showtime's' original series, The Big C.

The show starred Laura Linney and Oliver Platt and the basic premise was the journey of one woman's life as she dealt with impending death. Cathy Jamison, played by Laura Linney, a suburban wife, mother and high school teacher is diagnosed with stage 4 melanoma. The series followed her as she attempted to cope with the news, tell her family and live as well and as fully as possible to the end. For the sake of time, I've given you the Readers Digest version of the show. There is plenty to tell, great story lines and memorable characters played by Idris Elba, Susan Sarandon, Alan Alda, Brian Dennehy and Gabourey Sidibe to name a few.

Needless to say, the humor was sometimes dark and situations sad. Some people died very unexpectedly and others faded out of existence just as in real life. But the real triumphs were the choices Cathy made as she faced her death.

I'd like to believe I am capable of the courage, humor, strength and compassion Cathy showed throughout her ordeal. But I don't think I am. After all, Linney was playing a fictional character whose entire existence was written by someone who had the luxury of planning someone's demise. The show's creator had the comfort of knowing who would live, who would die and when. She knew what was going to happen in the future and the impact of each character that crossed Cathy's path. She knew when Cathy was going to die and how. She knew if Cathy would be alone or surrounded by family and friends. She knew it all. In essence, she was Cathy's version of God.

The rest of us are not so lucky but then again, maybe we are. Like Cathy, none of us really knows if our number is coming up today, a month, a year or a decade from now. We just know it is coming. We don't know who is going to go before us although we do know on that last day everyone we know who is alive is surely going after. We don't know what drink will be the last one, what movie will be the last one seen or if we are going to wake up the next day. We just assume we are because that's what makes life worth living.

Let's think about this for a moment. If you knew your actual expiration date, would you be jerking around with something you could have finished ages ago? If you knew you had a date with death at a specific time, would you be sitting around bitching about things or would you be out enjoying your family and friends? Would you try to travel to that place you've dreamed of or at least visit a museum or an art gallery or a restaurant that embodies that culture? Would you try to read every book you've wanted but couldn't find the time for? Would you take the time to try out a hobby or a sport that you've wanted to try?

The great thing about expiration dates is that it gives you a limit. As a journalist, I do my best writing when I'm on deadline. I'm extremely focused and the words seem to flow because I know my piece has to be turned in on time. That's why I set a deadline for my posts. It's a non-negotiable promise to my readers and promises are final. Without a deadline, I can piss off and never finish a single piece.

It's funny when you think about it, how much of what we do is governed by deadlines. Every bill you pay has a pay date. Every contract has a time limit. Our lives are governed by time. Job seniority, presidential terms, insurance policies, school – every facet of our lives is governed by a deadline and yet we live as though our time is unlimited. I've got a surprise for you, my friend. Time is unlimited. Your time is not. We all have an expiration date.

By now, you may be wondering where I'm going with this on time and death. I'm not really sure myself other than to give you and me a wakeup call. I do know I've wasted a lot of time on people, groups and situations that were unworthy of it. From now on, I intend to be more judicious about my precious commodity. I used to spend every day worrying about all the things I had to do and that there was not enough time to do them all. I used to feel guilty about taking a couple of hours to do nothing or do something I wanted to do. I used to spend sleepless nights worrying about what I hadn't done and what I needed to do. NO MORE!

What I'm choosing to do instead is spend my time doing more of the things I enjoy with the people I love. I'm going to do work that inspires me and helps others because that gives me joy. I'm going to watch the idiotic TV shows that make me laugh like World's Dumbest with no shame. I'm going to let the people I love know that I love them. I'm going to travel as much as I can and eat every cuisine I want. I'm going to take better care of this temple known as my body. I'm going to sit in the sun doing absolutely nothing for as long as I want, skin cancer be damned. I'm going to do all these things and more because I can. I may not be able to choose when and how and where I die. But I can certainly choose how I want to live just like The Big C's Cathy Jamison.

And my great hope for anyone who reads this is that you do the same. Great memories are not made about how we died but how we lived. I implore you. Live well!

Acknowledgment

Deepest thanks to my husband, **William Jerome Gibson**, parents **Charles & Eura Seavers**, brother **Darryl** and son, **Jeremey**.

Thanks to my dearest friends who give me strength, encouragement and a good kick in the ass when I need it: **Carolyn Binion, Loretta Campbell** and **Kevin Pierce**.

I like to thank **Bruce Moran** and **Corby Tate** of TotalRecall Publishing. Big thanks to the **National Writers Union UAW 1981** which I have been fortunate to have been a member of since 1994.

Thank you to my **blog readers**.

Finally, a special thanks to the wonderful women who have transitioned to the next life. They loved me, shaped me and help me to become the woman I am: **Mary Holmes Seavers, Mary E. Seavers, Brenda A. Cosey** and **Eyvonne Gaither**. I love them and miss them more than words can say.

www.ingramcontent.com/pod-product-compliance
Lightning Source LLC
Chambersburg PA
CBHW052059070526
44584CB00017B/2250